NOEMI LAN

The Ultimate
UK AIR FRYER
COOKBOOK
FOR BEGINNERS
2023

2000 Days Easy Breezy Air Fryer Recipes with a Guide to Innovative, Time-Saving, and Guilt-Free Cooking with Your Gadget I Recipe Book for Family

" Thank you.
This cookbook is dedicated to
my family and all your families.

Enjoy! "

TABLE OF CONTENT

$\mathcal{I}$NTRODUCTION

What is an Air Fryer

An Air Fryer is a kitchen appliance that cooks food by circulating hot air around it. This type of cooking method is also known as convection cooking. Air Fryers circulate hot air around the food, causing it to cook evenly on all sides. This cooking method is a healthier alternative to deep frying, using less oil and resulting in less greasy food. Air Fryers are becoming increasingly popular, as they are easy to use and can produce great results.

If you're thinking of buying an Air Fryer, here are a few things to keep in mind.

First, consider the size of the Air Fryer. Air Fryers come in various sizes, so choosing one that will fit your kitchen and meet your needs is essential. If you have a large family or entertain often, you'll need a larger Air Fryer. Second, think about the features you want. Some Air Fryers have features like timers and temperature controls, while others are more basic.

Decide what features are most important to you before making a purchase. Finally, consider your budget. Air Fryers range in price from around $30 to $200 or more, so it's essential to set a realistic budget before shopping. With these factors in mind, you're sure to find the perfect Air Fryer for your kitchen.

Air Fryers come in various sizes and features, but most have a basket or tray that holds the food and adjustable temperature control. Some models also have a timer so that the food can be cooked for the perfect amount of time. Air Fryers can be used to cook a variety of foods, including meats, vegetables, and even desserts.

Air Fryers have become a popular kitchen appliance in recent years, and for a good reason. An Air Fryer cooks crispy and delicious dishes with less oil than traditional frying methods. In addition to being healthier, air frying is also faster and more efficient, making it an excellent option for busy families or anyone who wants to save time in the kitchen. And because Air Fryers can be used to cook a wide variety of foods, from chicken wings to French fries, they are incredibly versatile and can help you create endless delicious meals. Whether you're looking to eat healthier or simply want to save time in the kitchen, an Air Fryer is a great option that will make your life easier.

An Air Fryer is a kitchen appliance that cooks food by circulating hot air around it. It is an alternative to deep frying in oil, which is believed to be healthier as it uses less oil. However, Air Fryers have other benefits too. For one, they can cook food faster than traditional methods. Additionally, Air Fryers can be used to cook various foods, not just the usual fried foods.

Features of Air Fryer

Here are 15 features of Air Fryers that make them a popular kitchen appliance:

1. They use less oil than traditional deep fryers.
2. They cook food faster than ovens or stovetops.
3. They are easy to use, and clean-up is simple.
4. You can cook various foods in an Air Fryer, including chicken, fish, vegetables, and desserts.
5. Air Fryers come in a variety of sizes to fit your needs.
6. Most Air Fryers have adjustable temperature settings so you can better control the cooking process.
7. Many Air Fryers have timers so you can set it and forget it until your food is done cooking.
8. Some higher-end models have automatic shut-off features for safety and peace of mind.
9. Some models include a window to check on your food without opening the basket and letting heat escape.
10. Most Air Fryers come with recipes or an introductory guide to start your cooking journey.
11. Some manufacturers offer customer support if you have questions or problems with your appliance.
12. Air Fryers are relatively affordable, with some models costing less than $100.
13. Air Fryers are widely available and can be purchased online or at most major retailers.
14. Air Fryer owners are delighted with their purchase, with many saying they would not go back to cooking without one!

Health Benefits of Air Fryers

Air Fryers have been gaining popularity in recent years as a healthier alternative to deep-frying. Unlike deep fryers, Air Fryers use little to no oil, instead relying on hot air to cook food. This can lead to significantly reduced calorie and fat content in fried foods. In addition, Air Fryers can cook food more evenly, resulting in a crispier exterior and a softer interior. Additionally, Air Fryers can be used to cook various foods, not just traditional fried foods. As a result, an Air Fryer can be a versatile and convenient appliance for any kitchen.

Air Fryers are kitchen appliances that many home cooks are beginning to use. An Air Fryer is a small countertop convection oven designed to cook food using little or no oil. Air Fryers work by circulating hot air around the food, which creates a crispy, fried texture without the need for unhealthy fats and oils. In addition to being a healthier cooking method, Air Fryers have many other benefits.

Here are ten reasons why you should consider using an Air Fryer in your kitchen:

1. Air Fryers cook food quickly and evenly.
2. They require less oil than traditional frying methods, making them a healthier option.
3. 5Air Fryers can be used to cook a variety of foods, including chicken, fish, vegetables, and even desserts.
4. They are easy to use and generally require little clean-up.
5. Many Air Fryers have built-in features, such as timers and temperature controls, that make cooking more accessible and foolproof.
6. Air Fryers are compact and take up very little counter space.
7. Air Fryers are relatively inexpensive, with some models costing less than $100.
8. Air Fryers can often be found second-hand at thrift stores or online sites like Craigslist or eBay.
9. An Air Fryer is worth considering if you want a healthier way to cook your food or simply want to try something new in the kitchen.

Health Benefits of Air Fryers

Air Fryers have become increasingly popular as people seek ways to eat healthier without sacrificing taste. And while some debate about the healthfulness of air-fried food, several benefits come with using an Air Fryer.

Here are ten health benefits of using an Air Fryer:

1. Air Fryers require little to no oil, which can help reduce your food's calorie and fat content.
2. Air Fryers cook food quickly, which can help to preserve nutrients.

3. Air Fryers can help make crispy foods without using unhealthy breading or batter.
4. Air Fryers can help reduce acrylamide's formation, a potentially cancer-causing compound that forms when starchy foods are cooked at high temperatures.
5. Air Fryers can kill harmful bacteria that may be present in food.
6. Air Fryers can cook frozen foods without the need for defrosting, which can reduce the risk of bacterial growth.
7. Air Fryers can help to reduce the amount of smoke and odours produced when cooking, making them a good option for those with respiratory conditions or sensitivities.
8. Air Fryers can be easier to clean than traditional ovens or frying pans, as they have fewer nooks and crannies for food to get stuck in.
9. Air Fryers are typically more energy-efficient than ovens, requiring less time to preheat and cook food.
10. While there is some debate about whether air-fried foods are truly healthy, they can be a healthier option than fried foods cooked in oil, as they contain less fat and calories overall.

Tips for cooking in Air Fryer

Here are ten tips to get the most out of your Air Fryer:

1. Don't forget o read the manufacturer's manual before you use your air fryer.
2. Preheat the Air Fryer before adding your food. This will help ensure that your food cooks evenly.
3. Cut food into uniform pieces. This will help them cook evenly and prevent them from sticking together.
4. Use high-quality cooking spray to grease Air Fryer.
5. Use a light coating of oil. This will help the food to crisp up without becoming greasy.
6. Shake or flip the food halfway through cooking. This will help it cook evenly on all sides.

7. Be careful not to overcrowd the Air Fryer basket. This will cause the food to be steamed instead of fried.
8. Preheat frozen foods before air frying. This will help them cook through more evenly.
9. Avoid using too much salt, as it can cause the food to stick to the basket or become overly salty.
10. Experiment with different seasonings and spices to find your perfect flavour combination.
11. Air-fried foods can overcook quickly, so keep an eye on them and check for doneness frequently.
12. Let cooked foods rest for a few minutes before serving to allow them to finish cooking and absorb any excess oil.
13. Don't delay cleaning after every cooking.
14. Make sure the air fryer is placed correctly before you start cooking.
15. Make sure to leave at least 4-inch of space from behind and above the Air fryer.

Cleaning and Maintenance

An Air Fryer is a kitchen appliance that cooks food by circulating hot air around it. It requires little to no oil, making it a healthier option than deep frying. As with any appliance, proper cleaning and maintenance are essential to keeping it in good working condition.

Here are some tips for cleaning and maintaining your Air Fryer:

- Empty the basket and drip tray after each use and wash them with warm soapy water.
- Make sure to use a soft sponge to clean the Air fryer.
- Wipe down the exterior of the Air Fryer with a damp cloth.
- Be sure to unplug the Air Fryer before cleaning it.
- Refer to the user manual for specific instructions on cleaning the appliance's interior.
- After cleaning of Air Fryer, make sure you store it safely.

Following these simple tips, you can keep your Air Fryer in excellent condition and enjoy delicious, healthy meals for years to come.

FAQs

1. What is an Air Fryer?

An Air Fryer is a small kitchen appliance that uses hot air to cook food. The food is placed in a basket inside the device, and hot air circulates it, cooking the food quickly and evenly.

2. How does an Air Fryer work?

An Air Fryer works by circulating hot air around the food in a basket inside the appliance. The hot air cooks the food quickly and evenly, producing a crispy and delicious dish.

3. What are the benefits of using an Air Fryer?

- Perfect cooking: The hot air circulated by the Air Fryer cooks food quickly and evenly, resulting in a perfectly cooked dish every time.
- Healthy cooking: Air frying uses little to no oil, making it a healthier option than deep frying.
- Versatile cooking: Air Fryers can be used to cook various foods, making them universal kitchen appliances.

4. What are some tips for using an Air Fryer?

- Here are some tips for using an Air Fryer:
- Preheat the appliance before adding food to ensure even cooking.
- Add food to the basket in small batches to prevent overcrowding.
- Shake or stir the basket occasionally during cooking to ensure even results.
- Use kitchen tongs or a fork to remove food from the basket, as it will be hot.

5. What are some common mistakes when using an Air Fryer?

- It is not preheating the appliance before adding food.
- They are overcrowding the basket.
- She is not shaking or stirring the basket during cooking.
- I am not using kitchen tongs or a fork to remove food from the basket.

These mistakes can result in unevenly cooked food or burned fingers! Following these tips will help you avoid these common mistakes and enjoy perfectly cooked food from your Air Fryer every time.

AIR FRYER
RECIPES

1. French Toast

Servings: 4	**Preparation Time:** 10 minutes	**Cooking Time:** 3 minutes

INGREDIENTS:

- Non-stick cooking spray
- Two eggs
- 3 tablespoons white sugar
- 60 millilitres of evaporated milk
- 2 teaspoons olive oil
- Dash of vanilla extract
- 4 bread slices

INSTRUCTIONS:

1. Grease the Air Fryer Pan with cooking spray and then slide inside.
2. Adjust the temperature of the Air Fryer to 200 °F to preheat for 5 minutes.
3. Press the "Start/Pause" button to start preheating.
4. Add all the ingredients except bread slices and mix well in a large bowl.
5. Coat the bread slices with egg mixture evenly.
6. After preheating, arrange the bread slices into the preheated Air Fryer Pan.
7. Slide the pan inside and set the time for 5 minutes.
8. Press the "Start/Pause" button to start cooking.
9. After 2½ minutes of cooking, press the "Start/Pause" button to pause cooking.
10. Flip the slices and press the "Start/Pause" button to resume cooking.
11. After cooking time is finished, remove the French toasts from Air Fryer and serve warm.

 Per Serving:
Calories: 165 | **Fat:** 5.8g | **Carbs:** 23.1g | **Protein:** 6.2g

2. Cheesy Toast with Egg & Bacon

 Servings:
4

 Preparation Time:
10 minutes

 Cooking Time:
5 minutes

INGREDIENTS:

- 113 grams ricotta cheese, crumbled
- 1 garlic clove, minced
- ¼ teaspoon lemon zest, grated
- Ground black pepper, as required
- 4 bread slices
- Non-stick cooking spray
- 2 hard-boiled eggs, peeled and chopped
- 4 cooked bacon slices, crumbled

INSTRUCTIONS:

1. In a food processor, add the ricotta, garlic, lemon zest and black pepper and pulse until smooth.
2. Spread ricotta mixture over each bread slice evenly.
3. Grease the Air Fryer Basket with cooking spray and then slide inside.
4. Adjust the temperature of the Air Fryer to 180 °C to preheat for 5 minutes.
5. Press the "Start/Pause" button to start preheating.
6. After preheating, arrange the bread slices into the Air Fryer Basket.
7. Slide the basket inside and set the time for 4 minutes.
8. Press "Start/Pause" button to start cooking.
9. After cooking time is finished, transfer the bread slices onto serving plates.
10. Top with egg and bacon pieces and serve.

Per Serving:
Calories: 416 | Fat: 29.3 | Carbs: 211.2g | Protein: 27.2g

3. Eggs in Avocado Cups

 Servings:
2

 Preparation Time:
10 minutes

 Cooking Time:
22 minutes

INGREDIENTS:

- 1 large ripe avocado, halved and pitted
- 2 eggs
- Salt and ground black pepper, as required
- Non-stick cooking spray
- 2 tablespoons Parmesan cheese, grated

INSTRUCTIONS:

1. With a spoon, scoop out some of the flesh from the avocado halves to make a hole.
2. Arrange the avocado halves onto a baking pan.
3. Crack one egg into each avocado half and sprinkle with salt and black pepper.
4. Grease the Air Fryer Basket with cooking spray and then slide inside.
5. Adjust the temperature of the Air Fryer to 180 °C to preheat for 5 minutes.
6. Press "Start/Pause" button to start preheating.
7. After preheating, arrange the avocado halves into the Air Fryer Basket.
8. Slide the basket inside and set the time for 22 minutes.
9. Press "Start/Pause" button to start cooking.
10. After 12 minutes of cooking, press "Start/Pause" button to pause cooking.

11. Sprinkle the top of avocado halves with Parmesan cheese and press the "Start/Pause" button to resume cooking.
12. After cooking time is finished, remove the avocado halves from Air Fryer.
13. Serve hot with the garnishing of chives.

 Per Serving:
Calories: 292 | Fat: 25.6g | Carbs: 9.3g | Protein: 9.9g

4. Bacon & Egg Cups

Servings:
2

Preparation Time:
10 minutes

Cooking Time:
8 minutes

INGREDIENTS:

- 1 cooked bacon slice, chopped
- 2 tablespoons milk
- 1 teaspoon marinara sauce
- 1 teaspoon fresh parsley, chopped
- 2 eggs
- Ground black pepper, as required
- 12 tablespoon Parmesan cheese, grated
- 2 bread slices, toasted and buttered

INSTRUCTIONS:

1. Slide the Air Fryer Basket inside and adjust the temperature to 180 °C to preheat for 5 minutes.
2. Press "Start/Pause" button to start preheating.
3. Divide the bacon into two ramekins.
4. Crack one egg in each ramekin over the bacon.
5. Pour the milk over the eggs and sprinkle with black pepper.

6. Top with marinara sauce, followed by the Parmesan cheese.
7. After preheating, arrange the ramekins into the Air Fryer Basket.
8. Slide the basket inside and set the time for 8 minutes.
9. Press "Start/Pause" button to start cooking.
10. After cooking time is finished, remove the ramekins from Air Fryer and sprinkle with parsley.
11. Serve hot alongside the bread slices.

 Per Serving:
Calories: 221 | Fat: 11.9g | Carbs: 13.2g | Protein: 15.5g

5. Broccoli & Egg Bites

Servings:
2

Preparation Time:
10 minutes

Cooking Time:
16 minutes

INGREDIENTS:

- Non-stick cooking spray
- 4 large eggs
- 1 teaspoon red pepper flakes, crushed
- Salt and ground black pepper, as required
- 80 grams broccoli, chopped

INSTRUCTIONS:

1. Grease 2 ramekins with cooking spray.
2. In a medium bowl, add the eggs, red pepper flakes, salt and black pepper and beat well.
3. Add the broccoli and stir to combine.
4. Divide the mixture into prepared ramekins evenly.

5. Slide the Air Fryer Basket inside and adjust the temperature to 180 ºC to preheat for 5 minutes.
6. Press "Start/Pause" button to start preheating.
7. After preheating, arrange the ramekins into the Air Fryer Basket.
8. Slide the basket inside and set the time for 16 minutes.
9. Press "Start/Pause" button to start cooking.
10. After cooking time is finished, remove the ramekins from Air Fryer and serve hot.

 Per Serving:
Calories: 165 | Fat: 10.5g | Carbs: 4.9g | Protein: 14g

6. Cream & Cheddar Omelette

 Servings: 2   **Preparation Time:** 10 minutes   **Cooking Time:** 8 minutes

INGREDIENTS:

- Non-stick cooking spray
- 4 eggs
- 60 grams of fresh cream
- Salt and ground black pepper, as required
- 30 grams cheddar cheese, grated

INSTRUCTIONS:

1. Lightly grease a 6x3-inch baking pan with cooking spray.
2. Add the eggs, cream, salt, and black pepper to a bowl and beat until well combined.

3. Place the egg mixture into the prepared pan.
4. Slide the Air Fryer Basket inside and adjust the temperature to 175 ºC to preheat for 5 minutes.
5. Press "Start/Pause" button to start preheating.
6. After preheating, arrange the baking pan into Air Fryer Basket.
7. Slide the basket inside and set the time for 8 minutes.
8. Press "Start/Pause" button to start cooking.
9. After 4 minutes of cooking, press "Start/Pause" button to pause cooking.
10. Sprinkle the cheese on the top of the omelette and again press the "Start/Pause" button to resume cooking.
11. After cooking time is finished, remove the baking pan from Air Fryer and transfer the omelette onto a plate.
12. Cut into equal-sized wedges and serve hot.

 Per Serving:
Calories: 263 | Fat: 20.45g | Carbs: 4.6g | Protein: 15.8g

7. Sausage & Bacon Omelet

 Servings: 2   **Preparation Time:** 10 minutes   **Cooking Time:** 10 minutes

INGREDIENTS:

- 4 eggs
- 2 sausages, chopped
- 1 bacon slice, chopped
- 1 yellow onion, chopped

- Non-stick cooking spray

INSTRUCTIONS:

1. In a bowl, whip the eggs well.
2. Add the remaining ingredients and gently stir to combine.
3. Place the mixture into a baking pan.
4. Grease the Air Fryer Basket with cooking spray and then slide inside.   Adjust the temperature of the Air Fryer to 160 °C to preheat for 5 minutes.
5. Press "Start/Pause" button to start preheating.
6. After preheating, arrange the baking pan in Air Fryer Basket.
7. Slide the basket inside and set the time for 10 minutes.
8. Press "Start/Pause" button to start cooking.
9. After cooking time is finished, remove the baking pan from Air Fryer and transfer the omelette onto a plate.
10. Cut into equal-sized wedges and serve hot.

Per Serving:
Calories: 500 | Fat: 38.4g | Carbs: 6g | Protein: 33.2g

8. Veggies Frittata

Servings:
2

Preparation Time:
15 minutes

Cooking Time:
18 minutes

INGREDIENTS:

- 60 grams half-and-half
- 4 large eggs
- Salt and ground black pepper, as required
- 60 grams fresh spinach, chopped
- 60 grams onion, chopped
- 50 grams tomato, chopped
- 55 grams feta cheese, crumbled
- Non-stick cooking spray

INSTRUCTIONS:

1. In a bowl, add the half-and-half, eggs, salt and black pepper and beat until well combined.
2. Add the spinach, onion, tomatoes and feta cheese and mix well.
3. Place the mixture into a baking pan.
4. Grease the Air Fryer Basket with cooking spray and then slide inside.   Adjust the temperature of the Air Fryer to 185 °C to preheat for 5 minutes.
5. Press "Start/Pause" button to start preheating.
6. After preheating, arrange the baking pan into Air Fryer Basket.
7. Slide the basket inside and set the time for 18 minutes.
8. Press "Start/Pause" button to start cooking.
9. After cooking time is finished, remove the baking pan from Air Fryer and place it onto a wire rack to cool for about 5 minutes before serving.

Per Serving:
Calories: 278 | Fat: 19.4g | Carbs: 8g | Protein: 18.8g

9. Turkey & Kale Frittata

Servings:
2

Preparation Time:
15 minutes

Cooking Time:
16 minutes

INGREDIENTS:

- 1 teaspoon olive oil
- 20 grams fresh kale, tough ribs removed and chopped
- ½ of tomato, cubed
- 35 grams cooked turkey meat, chopped
- 3 eggs
- Salt and ground black pepper, as required
- Non-stick cooking spray
- 30 grams Parmesan cheese, grated

INSTRUCTIONS:

1. In a non-stick skillet, heat the oil over medium heat and cook the kale for about 1-2 minutes.
2. Add the tomato and cook for about 2-3 minutes.
3. Remove from the heat and stir in the turkey. Set aside to cool slightly.
4. Meanwhile, in a small bowl, add the eggs, salt and black pepper and beat well.
5. Grease a baking dish with cooking spray.
6. In the prepared baking dish, place the turkey mixture and top with the eggs, followed by the cheese.
7. Slide the Air Fryer Basket inside and adjust the temperature to 180 ºC to preheat for 5 minutes.
8. Press "Start/Pause" button to start preheating.
9. After preheating, arrange the baking dish into the Air Fryer Basket.
10. Slide the basket inside and set the time for 8 minutes.
11. Press "Start/Pause" button to start cooking.
12. After cooking time is finished, remove the baking dish and place it on a wire rack for about 5 minutes before serving.

 Per Serving:

Calories: 199 | Fat: 13.1g | Carbs: 2.4g | Protein: 18.6g

10. Salmon Quiche

Servings:
2

Preparation Time:
15 minutes

Cooking Time:
20 minutes

INGREDIENTS:

- 155 grams salmon fillet, chopped
- Salt and ground black pepper, as required
- 2 teaspoons fresh lemon juice
- 1 egg yolk
- 50 grams of chilled butter
- 85 grams of white flour
- 3½ tablespoons cold water
- 2 eggs
- 45 grams of whipping cream
- 1 green onion, chopped

INSTRUCTIONS:

1. Mix the salmon, salt, black pepper, and lemon juice in a bowl. Set aside.
2. Add egg yolk, butter, flour, and water in another bowl and mix until a dough forms.
3. Place the dough onto a floured, smooth surface and roll into about a 7-inch round.
4. Place the dough in a quiche pan and press firmly in the bottom and along the edges. Trim the excess edges.
5. In a small bowl, add the eggs, cream, salt and black pepper and beat until well combined.
6. Place the cream mixture over the crust evenly and top with the chopped salmon, followed by the green onion.

7. Slide the Air Fryer Basket inside and adjust the temperature to 180 ºC to preheat for 5 minutes.
8. Press "Start/Pause" button to start preheating.
9. After preheating, arrange the quiche pan into the preheated Air Fryer Basket.
10. Slide the basket inside and set the time for 20 minutes.
11. Press "Start/Pause" button to start cooking.
12. After cooking time is finished, remove the quiche pan from Air Fryer and place it onto a wire rack to cool for about 5 minutes before serving.
13. Cut into equal-sized wedges and serve.

 Per Serving:
Calories: 596111 | **Fat:** 39.1g | **Carbs:** 34.4g | **Protein:** 27.2g

11. Sausage & Capsicum Casserole

 Servings: 6   **Preparation Time:** 15 minutes   **Cooking Time:** 25 minutes

INGREDIENTS:

- 1 teaspoon olive oil
- 455 grams of ground sausage
- 1 capsicum, seeded and chopped
- 30 grams onion, chopped
- 8 eggs, beaten
- 55 grams Colby Jack cheese, shredded
- ½ teaspoon garlic salt
- 1 teaspoon fennel seeds

INSTRUCTIONS:

1. Heat the oil over medium heat in a skillet and cook the sausage for about 4-5 minutes.
2. Add the capsicum and onion and cook for about 4-5 minutes.
3. Remove the heat and transfer the sausage mixture into a bowl to cool slightly.
4. In a baking pan, place the sausage mixture and top with the cheese, followed by the beaten eggs, fennel seeds and garlic salt.
5. Slide the Air Fryer Basket inside and adjust the temperature to 200 ºC to preheat for 5 minutes.
6. Press "Start/Pause" button to start preheating.
7. After preheating, arrange the baking pan into the Air Fryer Basket.
8. Slide the basket inside and set the time for 15 minutes.
9. Press "Start/Pause" button to start cooking.
10. After cooking time is finished, remove the baking pan from Air Fryer and set it aside for about 5 minutes.
11. Cut into equal-sized wedges and serve hot.

Per Serving:
Calories: 391 | **Fat:** 31.1g | **Carbs:** 2.5g | **Protein:** 24.4g

12. Raisin Muffins

 Servings: 4   **Preparation Time:** 10 minutes   **Cooking Time:** 10 minutes

INGREDIENTS:

- Non-stick cooking spray

- 65 grams of white flour
- 25 grams rolled oats
- 1/8 teaspoon baking powder
- 65 grams powdered sugar
- 113 grams butter, softened
- 2 eggs
- ¼ teaspoon vanilla extract
- 40 grams raisins

INSTRUCTIONS:

1. Grease 4 muffin moulds with cooking spray.
2. Mix the flour, oats, and baking powder in a bowl.
3. In another bowl, add the sugar and butter. Beat until you get the creamy texture.
4. Then, add the egg and vanilla extract and beat until well combined.
5. Add the egg mixture into the oat mixture and mix until just combined.
6. Fold in the raisins.
7. Place the mixture into the prepared muffin moulds evenly.
8. Slide e the Air Fryer Basket inside and adjust the temperature to 180 °C to preheat for 5 minutes.
9. Press "Start/Pause" button to start preheating.
10. After preheating, arrange the moulds into the Air Fryer Basket.
11. Slide the basket inside and set the time for 10 minutes.
12. Press "Start/Pause" button to start cooking.
13. After cooking time is finished, remove the moulds from Air Fryer and place them onto a wire rack to cool for about 10 minutes.
14. Then invert the muffins onto the wire rack to completely cool before serving.

Per Serving:
Calories: 409 | **Fat:** 25.7g | **Carbs:** 40.6g | **Protein:** 5.8g

13. Apple Muffins

 Servings: 12

 Preparation Time: 15 minutes

 Cooking Time: 25 minutes

INGREDIENTS:

- Non-stick cooking spray
- 230 grams of white flour
- 75 grams of white sugar
- 1½ teaspoons baking powder
- ½ teaspoon ground cinnamon
- ¼ teaspoon ground ginger
- ¼ teaspoon salt
- 180 millilitres milk
- 95 grams applesauce
- ¼ teaspoon vanilla essence
- 120 grams apple, cored and chopped

INSTRUCTIONS:

1. Grease 12 muffin moulds with cooking spray
2. Mix the flour, sugar, baking powder, spices, and salt in a large bowl.
3. Add in the milk, applesauce and vanilla essence and beat until combined.
4. Fold in the chopped apple.
5. Place the mixture evenly into the prepared muffin moulds.
6. Slide the Air Fryer Basket inside and adjust the temperature to 200 °C to preheat for 5 minutes.
7. Press "Start/Pause" button to start preheating.
8. After preheating, arrange the muffin moulds into the Air Fryer Basket.
9. Slide the basket inside and set the time for 20-25 minutes.
10. Press "Start/Pause" button to start cooking.

11. After cooking time is finished, remove the muffin moulds from Air Fryer and place them onto a wire rack to cool for about 10 minutes.
12. Then invert the muffins onto the wire rack to cool completely before serving.

 Per Serving:
Calories: 1101 | Fat: 0.2g | Carbs: 25.3g | Protein: 2.1g

14. Banana Bread

Servings:
8

Preparation Time:
10 minutes

Cooking Time:
20 minutes

INGREDIENTS:

- Non-stick cooking spray
- 200 grams of white flour
- 150 grams of white sugar
- 1 teaspoon baking soda
- 1 teaspoon baking powder
- One teaspoon of ground cinnamon
- 1 teaspoon salt
- 120 millilitres milk
- 120 millilitres olive oil
- Three bananas, peeled and sliced

INSTRUCTIONS:

1. Grease a loaf pan with cooking spray.
2. In a bowl of a stand mixer, add all the ingredients and mix well.
3. Place the mixture into the prepared loaf pan.
4. Slide the Air Fryer Basket inside and adjust the temperature to 165 °C to preheat for 5 minutes.

5. Press "Start/Pause" button to start preheating.
6. After preheating, arrange the loaf pan into the Air Fryer Basket.
7. Slide the basket inside and set the time for 20 minutes.
8. Press "Start/Pause" button to start cooking.
9. After cooking time is finished, remove the bread pan from Air Fryer and place the pan onto a wire rack for about 10-15 minutes.
10. Then invert the bread onto a wire rack to cool completely before slicing.
11. Cut the bread into desired-sized slices and serve.

 Per Serving:
Calories: 301 | Fat: 14.9g | Carbs: 41.1g | Protein: 3.6g

15. Date Bread

Servings:
10

Preparation Time:
15 minutes

Cooking Time:
22 minutes

INGREDIENTS:

- Non-stick cooking spray
- 435 grams dates, pitted and chopped
- 56 grams butter
- 240 millilitres hot water
- 195 grams of white flour
- 85 grams of brown sugar
- 1 teaspoon baking powder
- 1 teaspoon baking soda
- ½ teaspoon salt
- 1 egg

INSTRUCTIONS:

1. Grease a bread loaf pan with cooking spray.
2. In a large bowl, add the dates, butter and top with the hot water.
3. Set aside for about 5 minutes.
4. Mix the flour, brown sugar, baking powder, soda, and salt in a separate bowl.
5. In the same bowl of dates, add the flour mixture and egg and mix well.
6. Place the mixture into the prepared pan.
7. Slide the Air Fryer Basket inside and adjust the temperature to 170 ºC to preheat for 5 minutes.
8. Press "Start/Pause" button to start preheating.
9. After preheating, arrange the bread pans into the Air Fryer Basket.
10. Slide the basket into Air Fryer and set the time for 25 minutes.
11. Press "Start/Pause" button to start cooking.
12. After cooking time is finished, remove the bread pan from Air Fryer and place it on a wire rack for about 10-15 minutes.
13. Remove the bread from the pan and place it onto a wire rack until it is completely cool before slicing.
14. Cut the bread into desired size slices and serve.

 Per Serving:
Calories: 273 | Fat: 5.3g | Carbs: 56.1g | Protein: 3.7g

16. Herbed Cornish Game Hen

 Servings:
4

 Preparation Time:
15 minutes

 Cooking Time:
16 minutes

INGREDIENTS:

- 120 millilitres olive oil
- ½ teaspoon fresh thyme, chopped
- ½ teaspoon fresh rosemary, chopped
- ½ teaspoon fresh lemon zest, grated
- 1 teaspoon white sugar
- ¼ teaspoon red pepper flakes
- Salt and ground black pepper, as required
- 910 grams Cornish game hen, backbone removed and halved
- Non-stick cooking spray

INSTRUCTIONS:

1. Mix the oil, herbs, lemon zest, sugar, and spices in a bowl.
2. Add the hen portions and generously coat with the marinade.
3. Cover and refrigerate for about 24 hours.
4. In a strainer, place the hen portions aside to drain any liquid.
5. Grease the Air Fryer Basket with cooking spray and then slide inside.
6. Adjust the temperature to 200 °C to preheat for 5 minutes.
7. Press "Start/Pause" button to start preheating.
8. After preheating, arrange the hen portions into the Air Fryer Basket.
9. Slide the basket inside and set the time for 14-16 minutes.
10. Press "Start/Pause" button to start cooking.
11. After cooking time is finished, remove the hen portions from Air Fryer and place them onto a platter for about 5-10 minutes before serving.

 Per Serving:
Calories: 698 | Fat: 61.1g | Carbs: 2g | Protein: 38.7g

Poultry Recipes

02

17. Spiced Whole Chicken

 Servings: 6

 **Preparation Time:** 15 minutes

 Cooking Time: 1 hour

INGREDIENTS:

- ½ teaspoon dried thyme
- ½ teaspoon dried rosemary
- 2 teaspoons paprika
- One teaspoon of cayenne powder
- 1 teaspoon garlic powder
- 1 teaspoon onion powder
- 1 teaspoon ground white pepper
- Salt and ground black pepper, as required
- 3 tablespoons olive oil
- 1 (2¼-kilogram) whole chicken, necks and giblets removed
- Non-stick cooking spray

INSTRUCTIONS:

1. Mix the thyme, rosemary, spices, white pepper, salt and black pepper in a bowl.
2. Coat the chicken with oil and then rub it with a spice mixture.
3. Grease the Air Fryer Basket with cooking spray and then slide inside.
4. Adjust the temperature of the Air Fryer to 175 °C to preheat for 5 minutes.
5. Press "Start/Pause" button to start preheating.
6. After preheating, arrange the chicken into the Air Fryer Basket, breast side down.
7. Slide the basket inside and set the time for 60 minutes.
8. Press "Start/Pause" button to start cooking.
9. After 30 minutes of cooking, press "Start/Pause" button to pause cooking.
10. Flip the chicken and press the "Start/Pause" button to resume cooking.
11. After cooking time is finished, remove the chicken from Air Fryer and place it on a cutting board for about 10 minutes before carving.
12. Slice the chicken into desired size pieces and serve.

 Per Serving:
Calories: 781 | **Fat:** 54.4g | **Carbs:** 3.5g | **Protein:** 67.7g

18. Crispy Chicken Legs

 Servings: 3

 Preparation Time: 15 minutes

 Cooking Time: 20 minutes

INGREDIENTS:

- 3 (225-gram) chicken legs
- 240 millilitres buttermilk
- 130 grams of white flour
- ½ teaspoon onion powder
- ½ teaspoon garlic powder
- 1 teaspoon ground cumin
- 1 teaspoon paprika
- 1 teaspoon olive oil
- Salt and ground black pepper, as required
- Non-stick cooking spray

INSTRUCTIONS:

1. In a bowl, place the chicken legs and buttermilk and refrigerate for about 2 hours.
2. Mix the flour, spices, salt, and black pepper in a shallow dish.
3. Remove the chicken from the buttermilk.

4. Coat the chicken legs with flour mixture, dip into buttermilk, and coat with the flour mixture again.
5. Drizzle the chicken legs with the oil.
6. Grease the Air Fryer Basket with cooking spray and then slide inside.
7. Adjust the temperature of the Air Fryer to 185 °C to preheat for 5 minutes.
8. Press "Start/Pause" button to start preheating.
9. After preheating, arrange the chicken legs into the Air Fryer Basket.
10. Slide the basket inside and set the time for 20 minutes.
11. Press "Start/Pause" button to start cooking.
12. After cooking time is finished, remove the chicken legs from Air Fryer and serve hot.

 Per Serving:
Calories: 599 | Fat: 31.7g | Carbs: 38.2 | Protein: 43.4g

19. Sweet & Spicy Chicken Drumsticks

 Servings:
4

 Preparation Time:
10 minutes

 Cooking Time:
10 minutes

INGREDIENTS:

- 1 garlic clove, crushed
- 1 teaspoon olive oil
- 2 teaspoons mustard
- 2 teaspoons white sugar
- One teaspoon of red chilli powder
- 1 teaspoon cayenne powder
- Salt and ground black pepper, as required
- 4 (170-gram) chicken drumsticks
- Non-stick cooking spray

INSTRUCTIONS:

1. In a bowl, mix all ingredients except for chicken thighs.
2. Rub the chicken drumsticks with the oil mixture and refrigerate to marinate for about 20-30 minutes.
3. Grease the Air Fryer Basket with cooking spray and then slide inside.
4. Adjust the temperature of the Air Fryer to 200 °C to preheat for 5 minutes.
5. Press "Start/Pause" button to start preheating.
6. After preheating, arrange the chicken drumsticks into the Air Fryer Basket.
7. Slide the basket inside and set the time for 10 minutes.
8. Press "Start/Pause" button to start cooking.
9. After cooking time is finished, remove the chicken drumsticks and serve hot.

 Per Serving:
Calories: 360 | Fat: 15.1g | Carbs: 5.9g | Protein: 48.4g

20. Glazed Chicken Drumsticks

 Servings:
4

 Preparation Time:
10 minutes

 Cooking Time:
22 minutes

INGREDIENTS:

- 80 grams Dijon mustard
- 1 tablespoon honey
- 2 tablespoons olive oil
- 1 teaspoon fresh thyme, minced
- 1 teaspoon fresh rosemary, minced
- Salt and ground black pepper, as required
- 4 (150-grams) boneless chicken drumsticks
- Non-stick cooking spray

INSTRUCTIONS:

1. In a bowl, add the mustard, honey, oil, herbs, salt, and black pepper and mix well.
2. Add the drumsticks and generously coat them with the mixture.
3. Cover and refrigerate to marinate overnight.
4. Grease the Air Fryer Basket with cooking spray and then slide inside.
5. Adjust the temperature to 160 °C to preheat for 5 minutes.
6. Press "Start/Pause" button to start preheating.
7. After preheating, arrange the chicken drumsticks into the Air Fryer Basket in a single layer.
8. Slide the basket inside and set the time for 12 minutes
9. Press "Start/Pause" button to start cooking.
10. After 12 minutes of cooking, immediately adjust the temperature to 180 °C for 10 minutes.
11. After cooking time is finished, remove the chicken drumsticks from Air Fryer and serve hot.

 Per Serving:
Calories: 292 | Fat: 18.6g | Carbs: 5.8g | Protein: 25.1g

21. Lemony Chicken Thighs

 Servings: 4

 Preparation Time: 10 minutes

 Cooking Time: 20 minutes

INGREDIENTS:

- 4 (170-gram) boneless, skinless chicken thighs
- 2 tablespoons olive oil
- 2 tablespoons fresh lemon juice
- ½ teaspoon Italian seasoning
- Salt and ground black pepper, as required
- Non-stick cooking spray
- 1 lemon, sliced thinly

INSTRUCTIONS:

1. Add all the ingredients except for lemon slices and toss to coat well in a large bowl.
2. Refrigerate to marinate overnight.
3. Remove the chicken thighs and let any excess marinade drip off.
4. Grease the Air Fryer Basket with cooking spray and then slide inside.
5. Adjust the temperature of the Air Fryer to 175 °C to preheat for 5 minutes.
6. Press "Start/Pause" button to start preheating.
7. After preheating, arrange the chicken thighs into the Air Fryer Basket.
8. Slide the basket inside and set the time for 20 minutes.
9. Press "Start/Pause" button to start cooking.
10. After 10 minutes of cooking, press "Start/Pause" button to pause cooking.
11. Flip the chicken thighs and press the "Start/Pause" button to resume cooking.

12. After cooking time is finished, remove the chicken thighs from Air Fryer and serve hot alongside the lemon slices.

 Per Serving:
Calories: 367 | Fat: 17.5g | Carbs: 0.4g | Protein: 49.3g

22. Cheese-Stuffed Chicken Breasts

Servings:
4

Preparation Time:
15 minutes

Cooking Time:
15 minutes

INGREDIENTS:

- 2 (226-gram) skinless, boneless chicken breasts
- Salt and ground black pepper, as required
- 4 Brie cheese slices
- 1 tablespoon fresh chive, minced
- 4 cured ham slices
- Non-stick cooking spray

INSTRUCTIONS:

1. Cut each chicken breast into two equal-sized pieces.
2. Carefully, make a slit in each chicken piece horizontally about ¼-inch from the edge.
3. Open each chicken piece and season with salt and black pepper.
4. Place one cheese slice in the open area of each chicken piece and sprinkle with chives.
5. Close the chicken pieces and wrap each one with a ham slice.
6. Grease the Air Fryer Basket with cooking spray and then slide inside.

7. Adjust the temperature of the Air Fryer to 180 °C to preheat for 5 minutes.
8. Press "Start/Pause" button to start preheating.
9. After preheating, arrange the wrapped chicken pieces into the Air Fryer Basket in a single layer.
10. Slide the basket inside and set the time for 15 minutes.
11. Press "Start/Pause" button to start cooking.
12. After cooking time is finished, remove the chicken breasts from Air Fryer and serve hot.

 Per Serving:
Calories: 289 | Fat: 14.6g | Carbs: 2.2g | Protein: 35g

23. Bacon-Wrapped Chicken Breasts

Servings:
2

Preparation Time:
15 minutes

Cooking Time:
23 minutes

INGREDIENTS:

- 2 teaspoons palm sugar
- 6-7 Fresh basil leaves
- 2 tablespoons fish sauce
- 2 tablespoons water
- 2 (226-grams) chicken breasts, cut each breast in half horizontally
- Salt and ground black pepper, as required

- 12 bacon strips
- 1 tablespoon honey
- Non-stick cooking spray

INSTRUCTIONS:

1. Add palm sugar over medium-low heat in a small heavy-bottomed pan and cook for about 2-3 minutes or until caramelised, stirring continuously.
2. Add the basil, fish sauce and water and stir to combine.
3. Remove from heat and transfer the sugar mixture into a large bowl.
4. Sprinkle each chicken breast with salt and black pepper.
5. Add the chicken pieces into the bowl of sugar mixture and coat well.
6. Refrigerate to marinate for about 4-6 hours.
7. Wrap each chicken piece with three bacon strips.
8. Coat each piece with honey slightly.
9. Grease the Air Fryer Basket with cooking spray and then slide inside.
10. Adjust the temperature of the Air Fryer to 185 ºC to preheat for 5 minutes.
11. Press "Start/Pause" button to start preheating.
12. Arrange the chicken pieces into the Air Fryer Basket.
13. Slide the basket inside and set the time for 20 minutes.
14. Press "Start/Pause" button to start cooking.
15. After 10 minutes of cooking, press "Start/Pause" button to pause cooking.
16. To resume cooking, flip the chicken pieces and press the "Start/Pause" button.
17. After cooking time is finished, remove the chicken breasts from Air Fryer and serve hot.

Per Serving:
Calories: 365 | Fat: 24.9g | Carbs: 2.7g | Protein: 30.2g

24. Oat Crusted Chicken Breasts

Servings:
2

Preparation Time:
15 minutes

Cooking Time:
12 minutes

INGREDIENTS:

- 2 (150-grams) chicken breasts
- Salt and ground black pepper, as required
- 75 grams oats
- 20-30 grams of mustard powder
- 1 teaspoon fresh parsley
- 2 medium eggs
- Non-stick cooking spray

INSTRUCTIONS:

1. Place the chicken breasts onto a cutting board and flatten each with a meat mallet into even thicknesses.
2. Then, cut each breast in half.
3. Sprinkle the chicken pieces with salt and black pepper and set aside.
4. In a blender, add the oats, mustard powder, parsley, salt and black pepper and pulse until a coarse breadcrumb-like mixture is formed.
5. Transfer the oat mixture into a shallow bowl.
6. In another bowl, crack the eggs and beat well.

7. Coat the chicken with oats mixture and then dip into beaten eggs and again coat with the oats mixture.
8. Grease the Air Fryer Basket with cooking spray and then slide inside.
9. Adjust the temperature to 175 °C to preheat for 5 minutes.
10. Press "Start/Pause" button to start preheating.
11. After preheating, arrange the chicken breasts into the Air Fryer Basket in a single layer.
12. Slide the basket inside and set the time for 12 minutes.
13. Press "Start/Pause" button to start cooking.
14. After 6 minutes of cooking, press "Start/Pause" button to pause cooking.
15. Flip the chicken breasts and press the "Start/Pause" button to resume cooking.
16. After cooking time is finished, remove the chicken breasts from Air Fryer and serve hot.

 Per Serving:
Calories: 429 | Fat: 13.8g | Carbs: 29g | Protein: 45.1g

25. Parmesan Chicken Breasts

Servings:
3

Preparation Time:
15 minutes

Cooking Time:
20 minutes

INGREDIENTS:

- 1 egg, beaten
- 115 grams breadcrumbs
- 2 tablespoons vegetable oil
- 1 tablespoon fresh basil
- 3 (170-gram) chicken breasts
- Non-stick cooking spray
- 55 grams pasta sauce
- 30 grams Parmesan cheese, grated

INSTRUCTIONS:

1. In a shallow bowl, beat the egg.
2. Add the oil, breadcrumbs, and basil to another bowl until a crumbly mixture forms.
3. Dip each chicken breast into the beaten egg and coat it with the breadcrumb mixture.
4. Grease the Air Fryer Basket with cooking spray and then slide inside.
5. Adjust the temperature of the Air Fryer to 175 °C to preheat for 5 minutes.
6. Press "Start/Pause" button to start preheating.
7. After preheating, arrange chicken breasts into the greased basket.
8. Slide the basket inside and set the time for 20 minutes.
9. Press "Start/Pause" button to start cooking.
10. After 15 minutes of cooking, press "Start/Pause" button to pause cooking.
11. Spoon the pasta sauce over chicken breasts evenly and sprinkle with cheese.
12. Again, press "Start/Pause" button to resume cooking.
13. After cooking time is finished, remove the chicken breasts from Air Fryer and serve hot.

 Per Serving:
Calories: 593 | Fat: 26.5g | Carbs: 28.2g | Protein: 59.1g

26. Lemony Turkey Legs

 Servings: 2

 Preparation Time: 10 minutes

 Cooking Time: 30 minutes

INGREDIENTS:

- 2 garlic cloves, minced
- 1 teaspoon fresh rosemary, minced
- 1 teaspoon fresh lime zest, finely grated
- 2 tablespoons olive oil
- 1 tablespoon fresh lime juice
- Salt and ground black pepper, as required
- 2 turkey legs
- Non-stick cooking spray

INSTRUCTIONS:

1. Mix the garlic, rosemary, lime zest, oil, juice, salt, and black pepper in a large bowl.
2. Add the turkey legs and generously coat them with marinade.
3. Refrigerate to marinate for about 6-8 hours.
4. Grease the Air Fryer Basket with cooking spray and then slide inside.
5. Adjust the temperature of the Air Fryer to 175 °C to preheat for 5 minutes.
6. Press "Start/Pause" button to start preheating.
7. After preheating, arrange the turkey legs into the Air Fryer Basket.
8. Slide the basket inside and set the time for 30 minutes.
9. Press "Start/Pause" button to start cooking.
10. After 15 minutes of cooking, press "Start/Pause" button to pause cooking.
11. Flip the turkey legs and press the "Start/Pause" button to resume cooking.
12. After cooking time is finished, remove the turkey legs from Air Fryer and serve hot.

 Per Serving:
Calories: 458 | Fat: 29.5g | Carbs: 2.3g | Protein: 44.6g

27. Buttered Turkey Breast

 Servings: 10

 Preparation Time: 10 minutes

 Cooking Time: 45 minutes

INGREDIENTS:

- Non-stick cooking spray
- 1 (3 kilograms 640 grams) bone-in turkey breast
- Salt and ground black pepper, as required
- 30 grams unsalted butter, melted

INSTRUCTIONS:

1. Grease the Air Fryer Basket with cooking spray and then slide inside.
2. Adjust the temperature of the Air Fryer to 180 °C to preheat for 5 minutes.
3. Press "Start/Pause" button to start preheating.
4. Sprinkle the turkey breast with salt and black pepper and drizzle with butter evenly.

5. After preheating, arrange turkey breast into the Air Fryer Basket, skin side down.
6. Slide the basket inside and set the time for 45 minutes.
7. Press "Start/Pause" button to start cooking.
8. After 20 minutes of cooking, press "Start/Pause" button to pause cooking.
9. Flip the turkey breast and press the "Start/Pause" button to resume cooking.
10. After cooking time is finished, remove the turkey breast from Air Fryer and place it on a cutting board for about 10 minutes before slicing.
11. Cut the turkey breast into desired-sized slices and serve.

 Per Serving:
Calories: 720 | Fat: 9g | Carbs: 0g | Protein: 97.2g

28. Herbed Turkey Breast

Servings:
6

Preparation Time:
15 minutes

Cooking Time:
35 minutes

INGREDIENTS:

- ½ teaspoon dried rosemary, crushed
- ½ teaspoon dried thyme, crushed
- ½ teaspoon dried sage, crushed
- One teaspoon of dark brown sugar
- ½ teaspoon paprika
- ½ teaspoon garlic powder
- Salt and ground black pepper, as required
- 1 teaspoon olive oil

- 1 (1135-gram) bone-in, skin-on turkey breast
- Non-stick cooking spray

INSTRUCTIONS:

1. Mix the herbs, brown sugar, and spices in a bowl.
2. Coat the turkey breast evenly with oil and gently rub it with the herb mixture.
3. Grease the Air Fryer Basket with cooking spray and then slide inside.
4. Adjust the temperature to 185 °C to preheat for 5 minutes.
5. Press "Start/Pause" button to start preheating.
6. After preheating, arrange the turkey breast into the Air Fryer Basket, skin-side down.
7. Slide the basket inside and set the time for 35 minutes.
8. Press "Start/Pause" button to start cooking.
9. After 18 minutes of cooking, press "Start/Pause" button to pause cooking.
10. Flip the turkey breast and press the "Start/Pause" button to resume cooking.
11. After cooking time is finished, remove the turkey breast from Air Fryer and place it on a cutting board for about 10 minutes before slicing.
12. Cut the turkey breast into desired-sized slices and serve.

 Per Serving:
Calories: 349 | Fat: 16g | Carbs: 1.8g | Protein: 40.7g

29. Turkey & Salsa Meatloaf

Servings:
4

 Preparation Time:
15 minutes

 Cooking Time:
20 minutes

INGREDIENTS:

- 455 grams of ground turkey
- 115 grams of Monterey Jack cheese, grated
- 50 grams of fresh breadcrumbs
- 1 egg, beaten
- 65 grams salsa verde
- 55 grams of fresh kale, trimmed and finely chopped
- 50 grams onion, chopped
- 1 (113-gram) can of chopped green chillies
- 1 tablespoon fresh coriander, chopped
- 2 garlic cloves, minced
- ½ teaspoon dried oregano, crushed
- 1 teaspoon red chilli powder
- ½ teaspoon ground cumin
- Salt and ground black pepper, as required
- Non-stick cooking spray

INSTRUCTIONS:

1. In a deep bowl, place all the ingredients and mix until well combined with your hands.
2. Divide the turkey mixture into four equal-sized portions and shape each into a mini loaf.
3. Grease the Air Fryer Basket with cooking spray and then slide inside.
4. Adjust the temperature of the Air Fryer to 205 °C to preheat for 5 minutes.
5. Press "Start/Pause" button to start preheating.
6. After preheating, arrange the loaves into the Air Fryer Basket.

7. Slide the basket inside and set the time for 20 minutes.
8. Press "Start/Pause" button to start cooking.
9. After cooking time is finished, remove the loaves from Air Fryer and place them onto plates for about 5 minutes before serving.
10. Serve warm.

 Per Serving:
Calories: 429 | **Fat:** 18g | **Carbs:** 33.5g | **Protein:** 36.9g

30. Buttered Duck Breast

 Servings:
4

 Preparation Time:
15 minutes

 Cooking Time:
22 minutes

INGREDIENTS:

- 2 (340-gram) duck breasts
- Salt and ground black pepper, as required
- 28 grams unsalted butter, melted
- ½ teaspoon dried thyme, crushed
- ¼ teaspoon star anise powder
- Non-stick cooking spray

INSTRUCTIONS:

1. With a sharp knife, score the fat of duck breasts several times.
2. Season the duck breasts generously with salt and black pepper.
3. Grease the Air Fryer Basket with cooking spray and then slide inside.
4. Adjust the temperature of the Air Fryer to 200 °C to preheat for 5 minutes.
5. Press "Start/Pause" button to start preheating.

6. After preheating, arrange the duck breasts into the Air Fryer Basket.
7. Slide the basket inside and set the time for 22 minutes.
8. Press "Start/Pause" button to start cooking.
9. After 10 minutes of cooking, press "Start/Pause" button to pause cooking.
10. Remove duck breasts from the basket and coat with melted butter.
11. Then sprinkle with thyme and star anise powder.
12. Place duck breasts into the Air Fryer Basket and slide inside.
13. Again, press "Start/Pause" button to resume cooking.
14. After cooking time is finished, remove the duck breasts from Air Fryer and place them on a cutting board for about 5-10 minutes before slicing.
15. Cut each duck breast into desired size slices and serve.

....

 Per Serving:
Calories: 273 | **Fat:** 12.6g | **Carbs:** 0.8g | **Protein:** 37.6g

....

31. Bacon-Wrapped Filet Mignon

Servings:
2

Preparation Time:
10 minutes

Cooking Time:
15 minutes

INGREDIENTS:

- 2 bacon slices
- 2 (150-grams) filet mignon steaks
- Salt and ground black pepper, as required
- 1 teaspoon olive oil
- Non-stick cooking spray

INSTRUCTIONS:

1. Wrap one bacon slice around each mignon steak and secure with a toothpick.
2. Season the steak evenly with salt and black pepper
3. Then, coat each steak with avocado oil
4. Grease the Air Fryer Basket with cooking spray and then slide inside.
5. Adjust the temperature of the Air Fryer to 190 °C to preheat for 5 minutes.
6. Press "Start/Pause" button to start preheating.
7. After preheating, arrange the mignon steaks into the Air Fryer Basket.
8. Slide the basket inside and set the time for 15 minutes.
9. Press "Start/Pause" button to start cooking.
10. After 8 minutes of cooking, press "Start/Pause" button to pause cooking.
11. Flip the mignon steaks and press the "Start/Pause" button to resume cooking.
12. After cooking time is finished, remove the mignon steaks from Air Fryer and serve hot.

Per Serving:
Calories: 428 | Fat: 22.3g | Carbs: 0.5g | Protein: 52.9g

Red Meat Recipes

03

32. Crumbed Sirloin Steak

 Servings: 4 **Preparation Time:** 10 minutes **Cooking Time:** 10 minutes

INGREDIENTS:

- 130 grams of white flour
- 2 eggs
- 120 grams of panko breadcrumbs
- 2½ teaspoons onion powder
- 2½ teaspoons garlic powder
- ½ teaspoon paprika
- Salt and ground black pepper, as required
- 4 (170-gram) sirloin steaks, pounded slightly
- Non-stick cooking spray

INSTRUCTIONS:

1. In a shallow bowl, place the flour.
2. Crack the eggs in a second bowl and beat well.
3. In a third bowl, mix the panko and spices.
4. Coat each steak with the flour, then dip into beaten eggs and, finally, coat with panko mixture.
5. Grease the Air Fryer Basket with cooking spray and then slide inside.
6. Adjust the temperature of the Air Fryer to 185 °C to preheat for 5 minutes.
7. Press "Start/Pause" button to start preheating.
8. After preheating, arrange the steaks into Air Fryer Basket.
9. Slide the basket inside and set the time for 10 minutes.
10. Press "Start/Pause" button to start cooking.
11. After cooking time is finished, remove the steaks from Air Fryer and serve immediately.

 Per Serving:
Calories: 454 | Fat: 10.6g | Carbs: 31.8g | Protein: 37.2g

33. Buttered Rib-Eye-Steak

 Servings: 4 **Preparation Time:** 10 minutes **Cooking Time:** 14 minutes

INGREDIENTS:

- 113 grams unsalted butter, softened
- 1 teaspoon fresh parsley, chopped
- Two teaspoons of garlic, minced
- 1 teaspoon Worcestershire sauce
- Salt, as required
- 2 (226-grams) rib-eye steaks
- 1 teaspoon olive oil
- Ground black pepper, as required
- Non-stick cooking spray

INSTRUCTIONS:

1. Add the butter, parsley, garlic, Worcestershire sauce, and salt to a bowl and mix until well combined.
2. Place the butter mixture onto parchment paper and roll it into a log.
3. Refrigerate until using.
4. Coat the steak evenly with oil and sprinkle with salt and black pepper.
5. Grease the Air Fryer Basket with cooking spray and then slide inside.

6. Adjust the temperature of the Air Fryer to 205 °C to preheat for 5 minutes.
7. Press "Start/Pause" button to start preheating.
8. After preheating, arrange the steaks into the Air Fryer Basket.
9. Slide the basket inside and set the time for 14 minutes.
10. Press "Start/Pause" button to start cooking.
11. After 7 minutes of cooking, press "Start/Pause" button to pause cooking.
12. Flip the steaks and press the "Start/Pause" button to resume cooking.
13. After cooking time is finished, remove the steaks from Air Fryer and place them onto a platter for about 5 minutes.
14. Cut each steak into desired-sized slices and divide onto serving plates.
15. Now, cut the butter log into slices.
16. Top steak slices with butter slices and serve.

 Per Serving:
Calories: 459 | **Fat:** 36.5g | **Carbs:** 0.9g | **Protein:** 31.2g

34. Rosemary Beef Chuck Roast

Servings:
6

Preparation Time:
10 minutes

Cooking Time:
45 minutes

INGREDIENTS:

- 2 tablespoons olive oil
- One teaspoon of dried rosemary, crushed
- Salt, as required
- 1 (910-gram) beef chuck roast
- Non-stick cooking spray

INSTRUCTIONS:

1. Add the oil, rosemary, and salt to a bowl and mix well.
2. Coat the beef roast with rosemary mixture generously.
3. Grease the Air Fryer Basket with cooking spray and then slide inside.
4. Adjust the temperature of the Air Fryer to 180 °C to preheat for 5 minutes.
5. Press "Start/Pause" button to start preheating.
6. After preheating, arrange the roast into the Air Fryer Basket.
7. Slide the basket inside and set the time for 45 minutes.
8. Press "Start/Pause" button to start cooking.
9. After cooking time is finished, remove the roast and place it on a cutting board.
10. Cover the beef roast with a piece of foil for about 20 minutes before slicing.
11. Cut the beef roast into desired size slices and serve.

 Per Serving:
Calories: 424 | **Fat:** 24.7g | **Carbs:** 0.5g | **Protein:** 47.2g

35. Smoky Beef Burgers

Servings: 4

Preparation Time: 15 minutes

Cooking Time: 10 minutes

INGREDIENTS:

- 455 grams of ground beef
- 1 tablespoon Worcestershire sauce
- 1 teaspoon Maggi seasoning sauce
- 3-4 drops of liquid smoke
- ½ teaspoon dried parsley
- ½ teaspoon garlic powder
- Salt and ground black pepper, as required
- Olive oil cooking spray

INSTRUCTIONS:

1. Mix the beef, sauces, liquid smoke, parsley, garlic powder, salt, and black pepper in a large bowl.
2. Make four equal-sized patties from the mixture.
3. Grease the Air Fryer Basket with cooking spray and then slide inside.
4. Adjust the temperature of the Air Fryer to 175 °C to preheat for 5 minutes.
5. Press "Start/Pause" button to start preheating.
6. After reheating, arrange the patties into the air Fry Basket in a single layer.
7. With your thumb, make an indent in the centre of each patty and spray with cooking spray.
8. Slide the basket inside and set the time for 10 minutes.
9. Press "Start/Pause" button to start cooking.
10. After cooking time is finished, remove the patties from Air Fryer and serve hot.

Per Serving:

Calories: 220 | **Fat:** 7.1g | **Carbs:** 1.8g | **Protein:** 34.7g

36. Glazed Pork Tenderloin

Servings: 3

Preparation Time: 10 minutes

Cooking Time: 25 minutes

INGREDIENTS:

- 2 tablespoons Sriracha
- 35 grams honey
- Salt, as required
- 455 grams of pork tenderloin
- Non-stick cooking spray

INSTRUCTIONS:

1. Add the Sriracha, honey, and salt to a small bowl and mix well.
2. Brush the pork tenderloin with the honey mixture evenly.
3. Grease the Air Fryer Basket with cooking spray and then slide inside.
4. Adjust the temperature of the Air Fryer to 175 °C to preheat for 5 minutes.
5. Press "Start/Pause" button to start preheating.
6. After preheating, arrange the pork tenderloin into the Air Fryer Basket.
7. Slide the basket inside and set the time for 25 minutes.
8. Press "Start/Pause" button to start cooking.
9. After cooking time is finished, remove the pork tenderloin from Air Fryer and place it on a platter for about 10 minutes before slicing.

10. Cut the tenderloin into desired-sized slices and serve.

 Per Serving:
Calories: 263 | Fat: 5.3g | Carbs: 11.7g | Protein: 39.7g

37. Basil Pork Loin

Servings:
6

Preparation Time:
10 minutes

Cooking Time:
20 minutes

INGREDIENTS:

- 2 tablespoons white sugar
- 1 teaspoon dried basil
- 2½ teaspoons garlic powder
- Salt, as required
- 910 grams of pork loin
- Non-stick cooking spray

INSTRUCTIONS:

1. Add the sugar, basil, garlic powder, and salt to a bowl and mix well.
2. Rub the pork loin with the bail mixture generously.
3. Grease the Air Fryer Basket with cooking spray and then slide inside.
4. Adjust the Air Fryer to 210 °C to preheat for 5 minutes.
5. Press "Start/Pause" button to start preheating.
6. After preheating, arrange the pork loin into the Air Fryer Basket.
7. Slide the basket inside and set the time for 20 minutes.
8. Press "Start/Pause" button to start cooking.

9. After 10 minutes of cooking, press "Start/Pause" button to pause cooking.
10. Flip the pork loin and press the "Start/Pause" button to resume cooking.
11. After cooking time is finished, remove the pork loin and place the pork loin on a cutting board.
12. Cut into desired-sized slices and serve.

 Per Serving:
Calories: 386 | Fat: 21.1g | Carbs: 4.8g | Protein: 41.6g

38. BBQ Pork Chops

Servings:
6

Preparation Time:
10 minutes

Cooking Time:
16 minutes

INGREDIENTS:

- 6 (225-gram) pork loin chops
- Salt and ground black pepper, as required
- 115 grams of BBQ sauce
- Non-stick cooking spray

INSTRUCTIONS:

1. With a meat mallet, pound the chops thoroughly.
2. Sprinkle the chops with a bit of salt and black pepper.
3. Add the BBQ sauce and chops to a large bowl and mix well.
4. Refrigerate, covered for about 6-8 hours.
5. Remove the chops from the bowl and discard the excess sauce.
6. Grease the Air Fryer Basket with cooking spray and then slide inside.

7. Adjust the temperature of the Air Fryer to 180 °C to preheat for 5 minutes.
8. Press "Start/Pause" button to start preheating.
9. After preheating, arrange the pork chops into the Air Fryer Basket.
10. Slide the basket inside and set the time for 16 minutes.
11. Press "Start/Pause" button to start cooking.
12. After 8 minutes of cooking, press "Start/Pause" button to pause cooking.
13. Flip the chops and press the "Start/Pause" button to resume cooking.
14. After cooking time is finished, remove the chops from Air Fryer and serve hot.

 Per Serving:
Calories: 346 | Fat: 15.9g | Carbs: 8.3g | Protein: 38.4g

39. Feta Pork Meatballs

Servings:
8

Preparation Time:
15 minutes

Cooking Time:
24 minutes

INGREDIENTS:

- 910 grams of ground pork
- 1 medium onion, chopped roughly
- 15 grams fresh parsley, chopped roughly
- 4 garlic cloves, peeled
- 55 grams feta cheese, crumbled
- 75 grams of seasoned Italian breadcrumbs
- 2 eggs, lightly beaten
- Salt and ground black pepper, as required
- 1 tablespoon Worcestershire sauce

- Non-stick cooking spray

INSTRUCTIONS:

1. In a mini food processor, add the onion, parsley and garlic and pulse until finely chopped.
2. Transfer the onion mixture into a large bowl.
3. Add the remaining ingredients and mix until well combined.
4. Make equal-sized balls from the mixture.
5. Grease the Air Fryer Basket with cooking spray and then slide inside.
6. Adjust the Air Fryer to 210 °C to preheat for 5 minutes.
7. Press "Start/Pause" button to start preheating.
8. After preheating, arrange the meatballs into the Air Fryer Basket
9. Slide the basket inside and set the time for 12 minutes.
10. Press "Start/Pause" button to start cooking.
11. After cooking time is finished, remove the meatballs and serve hot.

 Per Serving:
Calories: 243 | Fat: 7.1g | Carbs: 9.1g | Protein: 33.8g

40. Honey-Mustard Glazed Ham

Servings:
4

Preparation Time:
10 minutes

Cooking Time:
40 minutes

INGREDIENTS:

- 755 grams ham
- 240 millilitres whiskey
- 2 tablespoons French mustard
- 2 tablespoons honey
- Non-stick cooking spray

INSTRUCTIONS:

1. Place the ham at room temperature for about 30 minutes before cooking.
2. In a bowl, mix the whiskey, mustard, and honey.
3. Place the ham in a baking dish that fits in the Air Fryer.
4. Top with half of the honey mixture and coat well.
5. Grease the Air Fryer Basket with cooking spray and then slide inside.
6. Adjust the temperature of the Air Fryer to 160 °C to preheat for 5 minutes.
7. Press "Start/Pause" button to start preheating.
8. After preheating, arrange the baking dish into the Air Fryer Basket.
9. Slide the basket inside and set the time for 40 minutes.
10. Press "Start/Pause" button to start cooking.
11. After 15 minutes of cooking, press "Start/Pause" button to pause cooking.
12. Flip the ham and top with the remaining honey mixture.
13. Again, press "Start/Pause" button to resume cooking.
14. After cooking time is finished, remove the ham from Air Fryer and place it on a platter for about 10 minutes before slicing.
15. Cut the ham into desired size slices and serve.

 Per Serving:

Calories: 515 | Fat: 17.8g | Carbs: 17.9g | Protein: 32.6g

41. Simple Lamb Chops

 Servings: 2 **Preparation Time:** 10 minutes **Cooking Time:** 6 minutes

INGREDIENTS:

- 1 teaspoon olive oil
- Salt and ground black pepper, as required
- 4 (115-gram) lamb chops
- Non-stick cooking spray

INSTRUCTIONS:

1. Mix the oil, salt, and black pepper in a large bowl.
2. Add the chops and coat evenly with the mixture.
3. Grease the Air Fryer Basket with cooking spray and then slide it inside
4. Adjust the temperature of the Air Fryer to 200 °C to preheat for 5 minutes.
5. Press "Start/Pause" button to start preheating.
6. After preheating, arrange chops into the Air Fryer Basket in a single layer.
7. Slide the basket inside and set the time for 6 minutes.
8. Press "Start/Pause" button to start cooking.
9. After cooking time is finished, remove the chops from Air Fryer and serve hot.

Per Serving:
Calories: 489 | Fat: 24g | Carbs: 0g | Protein: 64.6g

42. Herbed Lamb Chops

Servings:
2

Preparation Time:
10 minutes

Cooking Time:
7 minutes

INGREDIENTS:

- 1 tablespoon fresh lemon juice
- 1 teaspoon olive oil
- ½ teaspoon dried rosemary
- ½ teaspoon dried thyme
- ½ teaspoon ground coriander
- ½ teaspoon ground cumin
- Salt and ground black pepper, as required
- 4 (115-gram) lamb chops
- Non-stick cooking spray

INSTRUCTIONS:

1. Mix the lemon juice, oil, herbs, spices, salt, and black pepper in a bowl.
2. Add the chops and coat them with the herb mixture evenly.
3. Refrigerate to marinate for about 1 hour.
4. Grease the Air Fryer Basket with cooking spray and then slide inside.
5. Adjust the temperature of the Air Fryer to 200 °C to preheat for 5 minutes.
6. Press "Start/Pause" button to start preheating.
7. After preheating, arrange the chops into the Air Fryer Basket.
8. Slide the basket inside and set the time for 7 minutes.
9. After 4 minutes of cooking, press "Start/Pause" button to pause cooking.
10. Press "Start/Pause" button to start cooking.
11. Flip the chops and press the "Start/Pause" button to resume cooking.

12. After cooking time is finished, remove the chops from Air Fryer and serve hot.

 Per Serving:
Calories: 111 | Fat: 0.5g | Carbs: 27.1g | Protein: 1.5g

43. Pesto Rack of Lamb

Servings:
4

Preparation Time:
15 minutes

Cooking Time:
15 minutes

INGREDIENTS:

- ½ bunch of fresh mint
- 1 garlic clove, peeled
- 60 millilitres olive oil
- 1 tablespoon honey
- Salt and ground black pepper, as required
- 1 (680-grams) rack of lamb
- Non-stick cooking spray

INSTRUCTIONS:

1. For the pesto: in a blender, add the mint, garlic, oil, honey, salt, and black pepper and pulse until smooth.
2. Coat the rack of lamb with pesto evenly.
3. Grease the Air Fryer Basket with cooking spray and then slide inside.
4. Adjust the temperature of the Air Fryer to 95 °C to preheat for 5 minutes.
5. Press "Start/Pause" button to start preheating.
6. After preheating, place the rack of lamb into the prepared Air Fryer Basket.

7. Slide the basket into the Air Fryer and set the time for 15 minutes.
8. Press "Start/Pause" button to start cooking.
9. While cooking, coat the rack of lamb with the remaining pesto every 5 minutes.
10. After cooking time is finished, remove the rack of lamb from Air Fryer and place it on a cutting board for about 5 minutes.
11. Cut the rack into individual chops and serve.

 Per Serving:
Calories: 406 | **Fat:** 27.7g | **Carbs:** 2.9g | **Protein:** 34.9g

44. Herbed Leg of Lamb

Servings:
5

Preparation Time:
10 minutes

Cooking Time:
1¼ hours

INGREDIENTS:

- 907 grams bone-in leg of lamb
- 2 tablespoons olive oil
- Salt and ground black pepper, as required
- 2 fresh thyme sprigs
- 2 fresh rosemary sprigs
- Non-stick cooking spray

INSTRUCTIONS:

1. Coat the leg of lamb with oil and sprinkle with salt and black pepper.
2. Wrap the leg of lamb with herb sprigs.
3. Grease the Air Fryer Basket with cooking spray and then slide inside.
4. Adjust the temperature of the Air Fryer to 150 °C to preheat for 5 minutes.

5. Press "Start/Pause" button to start preheating.
6. After preheating, arrange the leg of lamb into the Air Fryer Basket.
7. Slide the basket inside and set the time for 75 minutes.
8. Press "Start/Pause" button to start cooking.
9. After 45 minutes of cooking, press "Start/Pause" button to pause cooking.
10. Flip the leg of the lamb and again press the "Start/Pause" button to resume cooking.
11. After cooking time is finished, remove the leg of lamb from Air Fryer and place it onto a platter.
12. Cover the leg of the lamb with a piece of foil for about 10 minutes before slicing.
13. Cut the leg of lamb into desired size pieces and serve.

 Per Serving:
Calories: 472 | **Fat:** 36.3g | **Carbs:** 1.4g | **Protein:** 32.3g

45. Leg of Lamb with Brussels Sprout

Servings:
6

Preparation Time:
15 minutes

Cooking Time:
1½ hours

INGREDIENTS:

- 925 grams leg of lamb
- 3 tablespoons olive oil, divided
- 1 tablespoon fresh rosemary, minced
- 1 teaspoon fresh lemon thyme

- 1 garlic clove, minced
- Salt and ground black pepper, as required
- Non-stick cooking spray
- 680 grams Brussels sprout, trimmed
- 3 tablespoons honey

INSTRUCTIONS:

1. With a sharp knife, score the leg of lamb in several places.
2. Mix 2 tablespoons of oil, herbs, garlic, salt, and black pepper in a bowl.
3. Generously coat the leg of lamb with an oil mixture.
4. Grease the Air Fryer Basket with cooking spray and then slide inside.
5. Adjust the temperature of the Air Fryer to 150 ºC to preheat for 5 minutes.
6. Press "Start/Pause" button to start preheating.
7. After preheating, arrange the leg of lamb into the Air Fryer Basket.
8. Slide the basket inside and set the time for 75 minutes.
9. Press "Start/Pause" button to start cooking.
10. Meanwhile, coat the Brussels sprout evenly with the remaining oil and honey.
11. After 75 minutes of cooking, press "Start/Pause" button to pause cooking.
12. Arrange the Brussels sprout around the leg of the lamb.
13. Slide the basket inside and immediately adjust the temperature of the Air Fryer to 200 ºC for 15 minutes.
14. Press "Start/Pause" button to resume cooking.
15. After cooking time is finished, remove the leg of lamb from Air Fryer and place it onto a platter.
16. Cover the leg of the lamb with a piece of foil for about 10 minutes before slicing.
17. Cut the leg of lamb into desired-sized pieces and serve alongside the Brussels sprout.

....

 Per Serving:
Calories: 417 | **Fat:** 18.9g | **Carbs:** 15.7g | **Protein:** 47.3g

....

46. Buttered Salmon

Servings:
2

Preparation Time:
10 minutes

Cooking Time:
10 minutes

INGREDIENTS:

- 2 (170-gram) salmon fillets
- Salt and ground black pepper, as required
- 1 tablespoon unsalted butter, melted
- Non-stick cooking spray

INSTRUCTIONS:

1. Season each salmon fillet with salt and black pepper and coat with the butter.
2. Grease the Air Fryer Basket with cooking spray and then slide inside.
3. Adjust the temperature of the Air Fryer to 185 °C to preheat for 5 minutes.
4. Press "Start/Pause" button to start preheating.
5. After preheating, arrange the salmon fillets into Air Fryer Basket.
6. Slide the basket inside and set the time for 10 minutes.
7. Press "Start/Pause" button to start cooking.
8. After cooking time is finished, remove the salmon fillets from Air Fryer and serve hot.

 Per Serving:
Calories: 286 | **Fat:** 17.6g | **Carbs:** 0g | **Protein:** 33g

47. Maple Salmon

Servings:
2

Preparation Time:
10 minutes

Cooking Time:
8 minutes

Fish & Seafood Recipes

04

INGREDIENTS:

- 2 (150-grams) salmon fillets
- Salt, as required
- 2 tablespoons maple syrup
- Non-stick cooking spray

INSTRUCTIONS:

1. Sprinkle the salmon fillets evenly with salt and coat them with maple syrup.
2. Grease the Air Fryer Basket with cooking spray and then slide inside.
3. Adjust the temperature to 180355 °C to preheat for 5 minutes.
4. Press "Start/Pause" button to start preheating.
5. After preheating, arrange the salmon fillets into the Air Fryer Basket in a single layer.
6. Slide the basket inside and set the time for 8 minutes.
7. Press "Start/Pause" button to start cooking.
8. After cooking time is finished, remove the salmon fillets from Air Fryer and serve hot.

 Per Serving:
Calories: 277 | **Fat:** 10.5g | **Carbs:** 13.4g | **Protein:** 33g

48. Spiced Salmon

Servings:
2

Preparation Time:
10 minutes

Cooking Time:
11 minutes

INGREDIENTS:

- 1 teaspoon cayenne powder
- ½ teaspoon smoked paprika
- ½ teaspoon garlic powder

- ½ teaspoon onion powder
- Salt and ground black pepper, as required
- 2 (150-gram) (3¾-centimeter thick) salmon fillets
- 2 teaspoons olive oil
- Non-stick cooking spray

INSTRUCTIONS:

1. Add the spices, salt and black pepper to a bowl and mix well.
2. Drizzle the salmon fillets with oil and then rub them with the spice mixture.
3. Grease the Air Fryer Basket with cooking spray and then slide inside.
4. Adjust the temperature to 390 °F to preheat for 5 minutes.
5. Press "Start/Pause" button to start preheating.
6. After preheating, arrange the salmon fillets into the Air Fryer Basket in a single layer.
7. Slide the basket inside and set the time for 11 minutes.
8. Press "Start/Pause" button to start cooking.
9. After cooking time is finished, remove the salmon fillets from Air Fryer and serve hot.

 Per Serving:
Calories: 278 | **Fat:** 15.4g | **Carbs:** 2.5g | **Protein:** 33.5g

49. Salmon with Broccoli

Servings:
2

Preparation Time:
15 minutes

Cooking Time:
12 minutes

INGREDIENTS:

- 135 grams small broccoli florets

- Two tablespoons of olive oil, divided
- Salt and ground black pepper, as required
- 1 tablespoon low-sodium soy sauce
- 1 teaspoon balsamic vinegar
- ½ teaspoon cornstarch
- ½ teaspoon white sugar
- 2 (170-gram) skin-on salmon fillets
- Non-stick cooking spray

INSTRUCTIONS:

1. Mix the broccoli, one tablespoon of oil, salt, and black pepper in a bowl.
2. Mix the remaining oil, soy sauce, vinegar, sugar, and cornstarch in another bowl.
3. Coat the salmon fillets with an oil mixture.
4. Grease the Air Fryer Basket with cooking spray and then slide inside.
5. Adjust the temperature of the Air Fryer to 190 ºC to preheat for 5 minutes.
6. Press "Start/Pause" button to start preheating.
7. After preheating, arrange the broccoli florets into the Air Fryer Basket.
8. Place the salmon fillets on top of broccoli, flesh-side down.
9. Slide the basket inside and set the time for 12 minutes.
10. Press "Start/Pause" button to start cooking.
11. After cooking time is finished, remove the salmon fillets and broccoli from Air Fryer and transfer them onto serving plates.
12. Serve hot.

 Per Serving:
Calories: 382 | Fat: 24.9g | Carbs: 7.4g | Protein: 35.4g

50. Salmon with Asparagus

Servings:	Preparation Time:	Cooking Time:
2	15 minutes	11 minutes

INGREDIENTS:

- 1 tablespoon fresh lemon juice
- 1 teaspoon olive oil
- 1 tablespoon fresh dill, chopped
- 1 tablespoon fresh parsley, chopped
- Salt and ground black pepper, as required
- 2 (170-gram) boneless salmon fillets
- 225 grams asparagus, trimmed

INSTRUCTIONS:

1. Add the lemon juice, oil, herbs, salt, and black pepper to a small bowl and mix well.
1. Mix the salmon and ¾ of the oil mixture in another large bowl.
2. In a second large bowl, add the asparagus and remaining oil mixture and mix well.
3. Grease the Air Fryer Basket with cooking spray and then slide inside.
4. Adjust the temperature to 210 ºC to preheat for 5 minutes.
5. Press "Start/Pause" button to start preheating.
6. After preheating, arrange the asparagus into the Air Fryer Basket.
7. Slide the basket inside and set the time for 11 minutes.
8. Press "Start/Pause" button to start cooking.
9. After 3 minutes of cooking, press "Start/Pause" button to pause cooking.
10. Place the salmon fillets on the asparagus and press the "Start/Pause" to resume cooking.

11. After cooking time is finished, remove the salmon fillets and asparagus from Air Fryer and serve hot.

 Per Serving:
Calories: 314 | **Fat:** 17.9g | **Carbs:** 5.2g | **Protein:** 35.8g

51. Cajun Catfish

Servings: 2

Preparation Time: 10 minutes

Cooking Time: 13 minutes

INGREDIENTS:

- Two tablespoons of cornmeal polenta
- 2 teaspoons Cajun seasoning
- ½ teaspoon paprika
- ½ teaspoon garlic powder
- Salt, as required
- 2 (170-gram) catfish fillets
- 1 teaspoon olive oil
- Non-stick cooking spray

INSTRUCTIONS:

1. Mix the cornmeal, Cajun seasoning, paprika, garlic powder, and salt in a bowl.
2. Add the catfish fillets and coat them evenly with the mixture.
3. Now, coat each fillet with oil.
4. Grease the Air Fryer Basket with cooking spray and then slide inside.
5. Adjust the temperature of the Air Fryer to 205 °C to preheat for 5 minutes.
6. Press "Start/Pause" button to start preheating.
7. After preheating, arrange the catfish fillets into the Air Fryer Basket in a single layer.
8. Slide the basket inside and set the time for 13 minutes.
9. Press "Start/Pause" button to start cooking.
10. After 7 minutes of cooking, press "Start/Pause" button to pause cooking.
11. Flip the catfish fillets and press the "Start/Pause" button to resume cooking.
12. After cooking time is finished, remove the fish fillets from Air Fryer and serve hot.

 Per Serving:
Calories: 335 | **Fat:** 20.3g | **Carbs:** 9.6g | **Protein:** 27.7g

52. Maple Glazed Hake

Servings: 4

Preparation Time: 10 minutes

Cooking Time: 12 minutes

INGREDIENTS:

- 70 grams of maple syrup
- 60 millilitres low-sodium soy sauce
- 1 tablespoon balsamic vinegar
- 1 teaspoon water
- 4 (115-gram) hake fillets
- Non-stick cooking spray

INSTRUCTIONS:

1. Mix the maple syrup, soy sauce, vinegar, and water in a small bowl.
2. In another small bowl, reserve about half of the mixture.
3. Add the hake fillets to the remaining mixture and coat well.

4. Cover the bowl and refrigerate to marinate for about 2 hours.
5. Grease the Air Fryer Basket with cooking spray and then slide inside.
6. Adjust the temperature of the Air Fryer to 180 °C to preheat for 5 minutes.
7. Press "Start/Pause" button to start preheating.
8. After preheating, arrange the hake fillets into the Air Fryer Basket.
9. Slide the basket inside and set the time for 12 minutes.
10. Press "Start/Pause" button to start cooking.
11. After cooking time is finished, remove the hake fillets and serve hot.

 Per Serving:
Calories: 153 | Fat: 2.3g | Carbs: 14.6g | Protein: 19.4g

53. Sesame Seed Tuna

Servings:
2

Preparation Time:
10 minutes

Cooking Time:
7 minutes

INGREDIENTS:

- 1 egg white
- 8 grams of black sesame seeds
- 30 grams of white sesame seeds
- Salt and ground black pepper, as required
- 2 (150-grams) tuna steaks
- Non-stick cooking spray

INSTRUCTIONS:

1. In a shallow bowl, beat the egg white.
2. Mix the sesame seeds, salt, and black pepper in another bowl.

3. Dip the tuna steaks into egg white and then coat with the sesame seeds mixture.
4. Grease the Air Fryer Basket with cooking spray and then slide inside.
5. Adjust the temperature of the Air Fryer to 205 °C to preheat for 5 minutes.
6. Press "Start/Pause" button to start preheating.
7. After preheating, arrange the tuna steaks into the Air Fryer Basket.
8. Slide the basket inside and set the time for 7 minutes.
9. Press "Start/Pause" button to start cooking.
10. After 4 minutes of cooking, press "Start/Pause" button to pause cooking.
11. Flip the tuna steaks and press the "Start/Pause" button.
12. After cooking time is finished, remove the tuna steaks from Air Fryer and serve hot.

 Per Serving:
Calories: 399 | Fat: 19.4g | Carbs: 4.8g | Protein: 50.2g

54. Crispy Cod

Servings:
4

Preparation Time:
15 minutes

Cooking Time:
15 minutes

INGREDIENTS:

- 4 (115-gram) cod fillets
- Salt, as required
- 2 tablespoons white flour
- 2 eggs
- 60 grams of panko breadcrumbs
- 1 teaspoon fresh dill, minced
- ½ teaspoon lemon zest, grated

- ½ teaspoon dry mustard
- ½ teaspoon paprika
- ½ teaspoon onion powder
- Non-stick cooking spray

INSTRUCTIONS:

1. Season the cod fillets with salt generously.
2. In a shallow bowl, place the flour.
3. Crack the eggs in a second bowl and beat well.
4. Mix the panko, dill, lemon zest, mustard, and spices in a third bowl.
5. Coat each cod fillet with the flour, dip into beaten eggs, and coat with panko mixture.
6. Grease the Air Fryer Basket with cooking spray and then slide inside.
7. Adjust the temperature of the Air Fryer to 205 °C to preheat for 5 minutes.
8. Press the "Start/Pause" button to start preheating.
9. After preheating, arrange the cod fillets into the Air Fryer Basket.
10. Spray the tops of fillets with cooking spray.
11. Slide the basket inside and set the time for 15 minutes.
12. Press the "Start/Pause" button to start cooking.
13. After 8 minutes of cooking, press "Start/Pause" button to pause cooking.
14. Flip the cod fillets and press the "Start/Pause" button to resume cooking.
15. After cooking time is finished, remove the cod fillets from Air Fryer and serve hot.

Per Serving:
Calories: 204 | Fat: 4.7g | Carbs: 6.9g | Protein: 24.6g

55. Breaded Flounder

Servings:	Preparation Time:	Cooking Time:
4	15 minutes	12 minutes

INGREDIENTS:

- 1 egg
- 120 grams of dry breadcrumbs
- 60 millilitres of vegetable oil
- 4 (170-gram) flounder fillets
- 1 lemon, sliced

INSTRUCTIONS:

1. In a shallow bowl, beat the egg
2. Add the breadcrumbs and oil to another bowl until a crumbly mixture is formed.
3. Dip flounder fillets into the beaten egg and coat them with the breadcrumb mixture.
4. Grease the Air Fryer Basket with cooking spray and then slide inside.
5. Adjust the temperature of the Air Fryer to 180 °C to preheat for 5 minutes.
6. Press the "Start/Pause" button to start preheating.
7. After preheating, arrange the flounder fillets into the Air Fryer Basket in a single layer.
8. Slide the basket inside and set the time for 12 minutes.
9. Press "Start/Pause" button to start cooking.
10. After cooking time is finished, remove the flounder fillets from Air Fryer and serve hot with the garnishing of lemon slices.

Per Serving:
Calories: 456 | Fat: 19.5g | Carbs: 21.7g | Protein: 43.4g

56. Ranch Tilapia

Servings: 4 **Preparation Time:** 15 minutes **Cooking Time:** 13 minutes

INGREDIENTS:

- 2 eggs
- 20 grams cornflakes, crushed
- 1 (28-grams) packet of dry ranch-style dressing mix
- 2 tablespoons vegetable oil
- 4 (150-grams) tilapia fillets
- Non-stick cooking spray

INSTRUCTIONS:

1. In a shallow bowl, beat the eggs.
2. Add the cornflakes, ranch dressing, and oil to another bowl until a crumbly mixture forms.
3. Dip the fish fillets into the egg and coat them with the breadcrumbs mixture.
4. Grease the Air Fryer Basket with cooking spray and then slide inside.
5. Adjust the temperature of the Air Fryer to 180 °C to preheat for 5 minutes.
6. Press the "Start/Pause" button to start preheating.
7. After preheating, arrange the tilapia fillets into the Air Fryer Basket.
8. Slide the basket inside and set the time for 13 minutes.
9. Press "Start/Pause" button to start cooking.
10. After cooking time is finished, remove the tilapia fillets and serve hot.

Per Serving:
Calories: 274 | **Fat:** 14.4g | **Carbs:** 4.9g | **Protein:** 31.1g

57. Shrimp Scampi

 Servings: 4 **Preparation Time:** 15 minutes **Cooking Time:** 7 minutes

INGREDIENTS:

- 40 grams of salted butter
- 1 tablespoon fresh lemon juice
- 2 teaspoons garlic, minced
- 1 teaspoon red pepper flakes, crushed
- 455 grams shrimp, peeled and deveined
- 1 teaspoon fresh basil, chopped
- 1 teaspoon fresh chives, chopped
- 1 tablespoon dry white wine

INSTRUCTIONS:

1. Arrange a 17½-centimeters round baking pan into the Air Fryer Basket.
2. Slide the Air Fryer Basket inside and adjust the temperature to 160 °C to preheat for 5 minutes.
3. Press the "Start/Pause" button to start preheating.
4. After preheating, place butter, lemon juice, garlic, and red pepper flakes into the heated baking pan and mix well.
5. Slide the basket inside and set the time for 7 minutes.
6. Press "Start/Pause" button to start cooking.
7. After 2 minutes of cooking, press "Start/Pause" button to pause cooking.
8. Add the shrimp, basil, chives and broth into the pan and stir to combine.
9. Again, press "Start/Pause" button to resume cooking.

10. After cooking time is finished, remove the baking pan from Air Fryer and place it on a wire rack for about 1 minute.
11. Stir the shrimp mixture and serve hot.

 Per Serving:
Calories: 221 | Fat: 10.5g | Carbs: 3.7g | Protein: 26.4g

58. Shrimp Kabobs

Servings:
2

Preparation Time:
15 minutes

Cooking Time:
8 minutes

INGREDIENTS:

- 2 tablespoons fresh lemon juice
- 1 teaspoon garlic, minced
- ½ teaspoon paprika
- ½ teaspoon ground cumin
- Salt and ground black pepper, as required
- 340 grams shrimp, peeled and deveined
- Non-stick cooking spray

INSTRUCTIONS:

1. Mix the lemon juice, garlic, and spices in a bowl.
2. Add the shrimp and mix well.
3. Thread the shrimp onto pre-soaked wooden skewers.
4. Grease the Air Fryer Basket with cooking spray and then slide it inside
5. Adjust the temperature to 350 °F to preheat for 5 minutes.
6. Press the "Start/Pause" button to start preheating.

7. After preheating, arrange the shrimp skewers into the Air Fryer Basket in a single layer.
8. Slide the basket inside and set the time for 8 minutes.
9. Press "Start/Pause" button to start cooking.
10. After 4 minutes of cooking, press "Start/Pause" button to pause cooking.
11. Flip the skewers and press the "Start/Pause" button to resume cooking.
12. After cooking time is finished, remove the shrimp skewers from Air Fryer and serve.

 Per Serving:
Calories: 212 | Fat: 3.2g | Carbs: 3.9g | Protein: 39.1g

59. Buttered Scallops

Servings:
2

Preparation Time:
15 minutes

Cooking Time:
4 minutes

INGREDIENTS:

- Non-stick cooking spray
- 340 grams sea scallops, cleaned and patted very dry
- 20 grams butter, melted
- 1 teaspoon fresh thyme
- Salt and ground black pepper, as required

INSTRUCTIONS:

1. Add the scallops, butter, thyme, salt, and black pepper to a large bowl. Toss to coat well.
2. Grease the Air Fryer Basket with cooking spray and then slide inside.

3. Adjust the temperature of the Air Fryer to 200 °C to preheat for 5 minutes.
4. Press the "Start/Pause" button to start preheating.
5. Arrange scallops into the Air Fryer Basket in a single layer.
6. Slide the basket inside and set the time for 4 minutes.
7. Press "Start/Pause" button to start cooking.
8. After cooking time is finished, remove the scallops from Air Fryer and serve hot.

 Per Serving:
Calories: 206 | **Fat:** 7.4g | **Carbs:** 4.7g | **Protein:** 28.7g

60. Scallops with Spinach

Servings:
2

Preparation Time:
15 minutes

Cooking Time:
10 minutes

INGREDIENTS:

- 1 (340-grams) package of frozen spinach, thawed and drained
- 8 jumbo sea scallops
- Non-stick cooking spray
- Salt and ground black pepper, as required
- 210 grams of heavy whipping cream
- 20 grams of tomato paste
- 1 teaspoon garlic, minced
- 1 teaspoon fresh basil, chopped

INSTRUCTIONS:

1. In a small baking pan, place the spinach.
2. Spray each scallop evenly with cooking spray and sprinkle with salt and black pepper.

3. Arrange scallops on top of the spinach in a single layer.
4. Add the cream, tomato paste, garlic, basil, salt, and black pepper to a bowl and mix well.
5. Place the cream mixture over the spinach and scallops evenly.
6. Slide the Air Fryer Basket inside and adjust the temperature to 175 °C to preheat for 5 minutes.
7. Press the "Start/Pause" button to start preheating.
8. After preheating, arrange the baking pan into the Air Fryer Basket.
9. Slide the basket inside and set the time for 10 minutes.
10. Press "Start/Pause" button to start cooking.
11. After cooking time is finished, remove the baking pan from Air Fryer and serve hot.

 Per Serving:
Calories: 203 | **Fat:** 18.3g | **Carbs:** 12.3g | **Protein:** 26.4g

61. Courgette Salad

Servings:
4

Preparation Time:
15 minutes

Cooking Time:
30 minutes

INGREDIENTS:

- 455 grams courgettes, cut into rounds
- 2 tablespoons olive oil
- Salt and ground black pepper, as required
- Non-stick cooking spray
- 150 grams fresh spinach, chopped
- 2 tablespoons fresh lemon juice
- 30 grams feta cheese, crumbled

INSTRUCTIONS:

1. Mix the courgette, oil, salt, and black pepper in a bowl.
2. Grease the Air Fryer Basket with cooking spray and then slide inside.
3. Adjust the Air Fryer to 210 °C to preheat for 5 minutes.
4. Press the "Start/Pause" button to start preheating.
5. After preheating, arrange the courgette slices into the Air Fryer Basket.
6. Slide the basket inside and set the time for 30 minutes.
7. Press "Start/Pause" button to start cooking.
8. While cooking, toss the courgette slices three times after every 8 minutes.
9. After cooking time is finished, remove the courgette slices from Air Fryer and place them onto a plate. Set aside to cool.
10. Add the cooked courgette slices, spinach, feta cheese, lemon juice, a little salt, and black pepper and toss to coat well.
11. Serve immediately.

Per Serving:
Calories: 109 | **Fat:** 9.1g | **Carbs:** 5.6g | **Protein:** 3.6g

Vegetarian Recipes

05

62. Brussels Sprout Salad

 Servings: 4 **Preparation Time:** 15 minutes **Cooking Time:** 14 minutes

INGREDIENTS:

For Salad:

- 455 grams medium Brussels sprout, trimmed and halved vertically
- 1 teaspoon olive oil
- Salt and ground black pepper, as required
- 2 apples, cored and chopped
- 1 red onion, sliced
- 300 grams lettuce, torn

For Dressing:

- 2 tablespoons olive oil
- 2 tablespoons fresh lemon juice
- 1 tablespoon honey
- 1 teaspoon Dijon mustard
- Salt and ground black pepper, as required

INSTRUCTIONS:

1. Grease the Air Fryer Basket with cooking spray and then slide inside.
2. Adjust the temperature of the Air Fryer to 185 °C to preheat for 5 minutes.
3. Press the "Start/Pause" button to start preheating.
4. For Brussels sprout: in a bowl, add the Brussels sprout, oil, salt, and black pepper and toss to coat well.
5. After preheating, arrange the Brussels sprout into the Air Fryer Basket.
6. Slide the basket inside and set the time for 15 minutes.
7. Press "Start/Pause" button to start cooking.
8. Flip the Brussels sprout once halfway through.
9. After cooking time is finished, remove the Brussels sprout from Air Fryer and transfer it onto a plate. Set aside to cool slightly.
10. Mix the Brussels sprout, apples, onion, and lettuce in a bowl.
11. For the dressing, add all the ingredients to a bowl and beat until well combined.
12. Place the dressing over the salad and toss to coat.
13. Serve immediately.

 Per Serving:
Calories: 298 | Fat: 11.5g | Carbs: 34.9g | Protein: 5g

63. Jacket Potatoes

 Servings: 2 **Preparation Time:** 15 minutes **Cooking Time:** 15 minutes

INGREDIENTS:

- 2 potatoes
- Non-stick cooking spray
- 45 grams of sour cream
- 1 tablespoon butter, softened
- 1 tablespoon mozzarella cheese, shredded
- 1 tablespoon fresh chives, minced
- Salt and ground black pepper, as required

INSTRUCTIONS:

1. With a fork, prick the potatoes.
2. Grease the Air Fryer Basket with cooking spray and then slide inside.
3. Adjust the temperature of the Air Fryer to 180 °C to preheat for 5 minutes.

4. Press "Start/Pause" button to start preheating.
5. After preheating, arrange the potatoes into the Air Fryer Basket.
6. Slide the basket inside and set the time for 15 minutes.
7. Press "Start/Pause" button to start cooking.
8. Meanwhile, in a bowl, add the remaining ingredients and mix until well combined.
9. After cooking time is finished, remove the potatoes from Air Fryer and transfer them onto a platter.
10. Open potatoes from the centre and stuff them with cheese mixture.
11. Serve immediately.

Per Serving:
Calories: 254 | **Fat:** 15.8g | **Carbs:** 28.9g | **Protein:** 1.2g

64. Caramelised Carrots

 Servings: 6   **Preparation Time:** 10 minutes 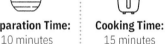 **Cooking Time:** 15 minutes

INGREDIENTS:

- Non-stick cooking spray
- 115 grams butter, melted
- 100 grams of brown sugar
- 1 (910-gram) bag of baby carrots

INSTRUCTIONS:

1. Grease the Air Fryer Basket with cooking spray and then slide inside.
2. Adjust the temperature to 204 °C to preheat for 5 minutes.

3. Press "Start/Pause" button to start preheating.
4. In a bowl, mix the butter and brown sugar
5. Add the carrots and coat well.
6. After preheating, arrange the carrots into the Air Fryer Basket in a single layer.
7. Slide the basket inside and set the time for 15 minutes.
8. Press "Start/Pause" button to start cooking.
9. After cooking time is finished, remove the carrots from Air Fryer and serve hot.

Per Serving:
Calories: 169 | **Fat:** 7.6g | **Carbs:** 20.2g | **Protein:** 9.7g

65. Parmesan Brussels Sprout

 Servings: 4   **Preparation Time:** 15 minutes   **Cooking Time:** 10 minutes

INGREDIENTS:

- Non-stick cooking spray
- 455 grams Brussels sprout, trimmed and halved
- 1 tablespoon balsamic vinegar
- 1 teaspoon olive oil
- Salt and ground black pepper, as required
- 25 grams breadcrumbs
- 30 grams Parmesan cheese, shredded

INSTRUCTIONS:

1. Grease the Air Fryer Basket with cooking spray and then slide inside.
2. Adjust the temperature to 205 °C to preheat for 5 minutes.
3. Press "Start/Pause" button to start preheating.
4. Mix Brussels sprout, vinegar, oil, salt, and black pepper in a bowl.
5. After preheating, arrange the Brussels sprout into the Air Fryer Basket in a single layer.
6. Slide the basket inside and set the time for 10 minutes.
7. Press "Start/Pause" button to start cooking.
8. After 5 minutes of cooking, press "Start/Pause" button to pause cooking.
9. Flip the Brussels sprout and sprinkle with breadcrumbs, followed by the cheese.
10. Again, press "Start/Pause" button to resume cooking.
11. After cooking time is finished, remove the Brussels sprout from Air Fryer and serve hot.

....

Per Serving:
Calories: 169 | **Fat:** 7.6g | **Carbs:** 20.2g | **Protein:** 9.7g

....

66. Goat Cheese Kale

 Servings: 4

 Preparation Time: 15 minutes

 Cooking Time: 15 minutes

INGREDIENTS:

- 455 grams fresh kale, tough ribs removed and chopped
- 110 grams goat cheese, crumbled
- 1 teaspoon fresh lemon juice
- 3 tablespoons olive oil
- Salt and ground black pepper, as required
- Non-stick cooking spray

INSTRUCTIONS:

1. Add the kale, oil, salt, and black pepper to a bowl and mix well.
2. Grease the Air Fryer Basket with cooking spray and then slide inside.
3. Adjust the temperature to 170°C to preheat for 5 minutes.
4. Press "Start/Pause" button to start preheating.
5. After preheating, arrange the kale into Air Fryer Basket.
6. Slide the basket into Air Fryer and set the time for 15 minutes.
7. Press "Start/Pause" button to start cooking.
8. After cooking time is finished, remove the kale mixture from Air Fryer and transfer it into a bowl.
9. Immediately stir in the cheese and lemon juice.
10. Serve hot.

....

 Per Serving:
Calories: 272 | **Fat:** 20.5g | **Carbs:** 12.5g | **Protein:** 11.8g

....

67. Feta Spinach

Servings:
6

Preparation Time:
15 minutes

Cooking Time:
15 minutes

68. Ratatouille

Servings:
4

Preparation Time:
15 minutes

Cooking Time:
15 minutes

INGREDIENTS:

- 910 grams fresh spinach, chopped
- 1 garlic clove, minced
- 1 jalapeño pepper, minced
- 40 grams butter, melted
- Salt and ground black pepper, as required
- 110 grams feta cheese, crumbled
- 1 teaspoon lemon zest, grated

INSTRUCTIONS:

1. In a bowl, add the spinach, garlic, jalapeño, butter, salt and black pepper and mix well.
2. Grease the Air Fryer Basket with cooking spray and then slide inside.
3. Adjust the temperature of the Air Fryer to 170 °C to preheat for 5 minutes.
4. Press "Start/Pause" button to start preheating.
5. After preheating, arrange the spinach mixture into the Air Fryer Basket.
6. Slide the basket inside and set the time for 15 minutes.
7. Press "Start/Pause" button to start cooking.
8. After cooking time is finished, remove the spinach mixture from Air Fryer and transfer it into a bowl.
9. Immediately stir in the cheese and lemon zest and serve hot.

....

 Per Serving:
Calories: 153 | Fat: 12.2g | Carbs: 6.7g | Protein: 7.1g

....

INGREDIENTS:

- Non-stick cooking spray
- 1 green capsicum, seeded and chopped
- 1 yellow capsicum, seeded and chopped
- 1 brinjal, chopped
- 1 courgette, chopped
- 3 tomatoes, chopped
- 2 small onions, chopped
- 2 garlic cloves, minced
- 2 tablespoons Herbs de Provence
- 1 teaspoon olive oil
- 1 tablespoon balsamic vinegar
- Salt and ground black pepper, as required

INSTRUCTIONS:

1. Grease a baking pan with cooking spray.
2. Add the vegetables, garlic, Herbs de Provence, oil, vinegar, salt, and black pepper to a large bowl and toss to coat well.
3. Place the vegetable mixture into the prepared baking pan.
4. Slide the Air Fryer Basket inside and adjust the temperature to 180 °C to preheat for 5 minutes.
5. Press "Start/Pause" button to start preheating.
6. After preheating, arrange the baking pan into the Air Fryer Basket.
7. Slide the basket inside and set the time for 15 minutes.
8. Press "Start/Pause" button to start cooking.

9. After cooking time is finished, remove the baking pan from Air Fryer and serve hot.

 Per Serving:
Calories: 120 | **Fat:** 4.2g | **Carbs:** 20.3g | **Protein:** 3.6g

69. Veggie Casserole

Servings:
6

Preparation Time:
15 minutes

Cooking Time:
12 minutes

INGREDIENTS:

- 680 grams of fresh green beans, trimmed
- 220 grams of fresh button mushrooms, sliced
- 60 millilitres of fresh lemon juice
- 3 tablespoons olive oil
- 1 teaspoon ground sage
- ½ teaspoon onion powder
- ½ teaspoon garlic powder
- 65 grams French fried onions

INSTRUCTIONS:

1. Add the green beans, mushrooms, lemon juice, oil, sage, and spices to a bowl and toss to coat well.
2. Slide the Air Fryer Basket inside and adjust the temperature to 205 °C to preheat for 5 minutes.
3. Press "Start/Pause" button to start preheating.
4. After preheating, arrange the mushroom mixture into the Air Fryer Basket.
5. Slide the basket inside and set the time for 10-12 minutes
6. Press "Start/Pause" button to start cooking.

7. While cooking, shake the basket several times.
8. After cooking time is finished, remove the mushroom mixture from Air Fryer and transfer it into a serving dish.
9. Top with fried onions and serve.

 Per Serving:
Calories: 184 | **Fat:** 12.2g | **Carbs:** 15.9g | **Protein:** 3.6g

70. Stuffed Pumpkin

Servings:
4

Preparation Time:
15 minutes

Cooking Time:
30 minutes

INGREDIENTS:

- 1 sweet potato, peeled and chopped
- 1 parsnip, peeled and chopped
- 1 carrot, peeled and chopped
- 70 grams fresh green peas, shelled
- 1 onion, chopped
- 2 garlic cloves, minced
- 1 egg, beaten
- 1 teaspoon mixed dried herbs
- Salt and ground black pepper, as required
- ½ of butternut pumpkin, seeded
- Non-stick cooking spray

INSTRUCTIONS:

1. Add vegetables, garlic, egg, herbs, salt, and black pepper to a large bowl and mix well.
2. Stuff the pumpkin half with vegetable mixture.
3. Grease the Air Fryer Basket with cooking spray and then slide inside.

4. Adjust the temperature of the Air Fryer to 180 °C to preheat for 5 minutes.
5. Press "Start/Pause" button to start preheating.
6. After preheating, arrange the pumpkin half into the prepared Air Fryer Basket.
7. Slide the basket inside and set the time for 30 minutes.
8. Press "Start/Pause" button to start cooking.
9. After cooking time is finished, remove the pumpkin from Air Fryer and place it onto a serving platter.
10. Set aside to cool slightly.
11. Serve warm.

 Per Serving:
Calories: 217 | **Fat:** 1.6g | **Carbs:** 49.4g | **Protein:** 6.6g

71. Stuffed Capsicum

 Servings:
4

 Preparation Time:
15 minutes

 Cooking Time:
16 minutes

INGREDIENTS:

- Non-stick cooking spray
- 2 large capsicums, halved lengthwise and seeded
- 320 grams of cooked oatmeal
- 55 grams canned red kidney beans, drained
- 70 grams of coconut yoghurt
- ¼ teaspoon smoked paprika
- ¼ teaspoon ground cumin
- Salt and ground black pepper, as required

INSTRUCTIONS:

1. Grease the Air Fryer Basket with cooking spray and then slide inside.
2. Adjust the temperature to 180 °C to preheat for 5 minutes.
3. Press "Start/Pause" button to start preheating.
4. After preheating, arrange the capsicums into the Air Fryer Basket, cut-side down.
5. Slide the basket inside and set the time for 8 minutes.
6. After cooking time is finished, remove the capsicums from Air Fryer and set them aside to cool.
7. Meanwhile, mix oatmeal, beans, coconut yoghurt, and spices in a bowl.
8. Stuff each capsicum half with the oatmeal mixture.
9. Again, grease the Air Fryer Basket with cooking spray and slide inside.
10. Adjust the temperature to 180 °C to preheat for 5 minutes.
11. Press "Start/Pause" button to start preheating.
12. After preheating, arrange the stuffed capsicums into the Air Fryer Basket.
13. Slide the basket inside and set the time for 8 minutes.
14. Press "Start/Pause" button to start cooking.
15. After cooking time is finished, remove the capsicums from Air Fryer and place them onto a serving platter.
16. Set aside to cool slightly before serving.

 Per Serving:
Calories: 214 | **Fat:** 4.1g | **Carbs:** 36.8g | **Protein:** 9.7g

72. Tofu with Cauliflower

Servings:
2

 Preparation Time:
15 minutes

 Cooking Time:
15 minutes

73. Tofu with Broccoli

 Servings:
2

 Preparation Time:
15 minutes

 Cooking Time:
15 minutes

INGREDIENTS:

- 1½ (1113-grams) block firm tofu, pressed and cubed
- 1 tablespoon nutritional yeast
- 1 teaspoon ground turmeric
- Salt and ground black pepper, as required
- ½ of small head cauliflower, cut into florets
- 1 tablespoon canola oil
- ¼ teaspoon dried parsley
- ¼ teaspoon paprika
- Non-stick cooking spray

INSTRUCTIONS:

1. Add tofu, cauliflower, and the remaining ingredients to a bowl and mix well.
2. Grease the Air Fryer Basket with cooking spray and then slide inside.
3. Adjust the temperature to 200 °C to preheat for 5 minutes.
4. Press "Start/Pause" button to start preheating.
5. After preheating, arrange the tofu mixture into the Air Fryer Basket in a single layer.
6. Slide the basket inside and set the time for 12–15 minutes.
7. Press "Start/Pause" button to start cooking.
8. While cooking, shake the basket once halfway through.
9. After cooking time is finished, remove the tofu from Air Fryer and serve hot.

Per Serving:
Calories: 170 | Fat: 11.9g | Carbs: 8.3g | Protein: 11.6g

INGREDIENTS:

- 226 grams of firm tofu, drained, pressed and cubed
- ½ head broccoli, cut into florets
- 1 teaspoon olive oil
- 1 teaspoon ground turmeric
- ¼ teaspoon paprika
- Salt and ground black pepper, as required
- Non-stick cooking spray

INSTRUCTIONS:

1. In a bowl, mix all ingredients.
2. Grease the Air Fryer Basket with cooking spray and then slide inside.
3. Adjust the temperature of the Air Fryer to 400 °C to preheat for 5 minutes.
4. Press "Start/Pause" button to start preheating.
5. After preheating, arrange the tofu mixture into the Air Fryer Basket.
6. Slide the basket inside and set the time for 15 minutes.
7. Press "Start/Pause" button to start cooking.
8. While cooking, shake the basket once halfway through.
9. After cooking time is finished, remove the tofu from Air Fryer and serve hot.

Per Serving:
Calories: 175 | Fat: 12.4g | Carbs: 8.6g | Protein: 11.5g

74. Black Beans Burgers

Servings:
4

Preparation Time:
15 minutes

Cooking Time:
21 minutes

INGREDIENTS:

- 175 grams of cooked black beans
- 330 grams boiled potatoes, peeled and mashed
- 30 grams fresh spinach, chopped
- 100 grams of fresh mushrooms, chopped
- 2 teaspoons Chile lime seasoning
- Non-stick cooking spray

INSTRUCTIONS:

1. In a large bowl, add the black beans, potatoes, spinach, mushrooms, and seasoning, and with your hands, mix until well combined.
2. Make 4 equal-sized patties from the mixture.
3. Grease the Air Fryer Basket with cooking spray and then slide inside.
4. Adjust the temperature of the Air Fryer to 190 °C to preheat for 5 minutes.
5. Press "Start/Pause" button to start preheating.
6. After preheating, arrange the patties into the Air Fryer Basket in a single layer and spray with the cooking spray.
7. Slide the basket inside and set the time for 18 minutes.
8. Press "Start/Pause" button to start cooking.
9. After 12 minutes of cooking, press "Start/Pause" button to pause cooking.
10. Flip the patties and spray with the cooking spray.
11. Again, press "Start/Pause" button to resume cooking.
12. After 18 minutes of cooking, adjust the temperature to 200 °C for 3 minutes.
13. After cooking time is finished, remove the burgers from Air Fryer and serve hot.

 Per Serving:
Calories: 121 | **Fat:** 0.4g | **Carbs:** 24.3g | **Protein:** 26.2g

75. Veggie Rice

Servings:
3

Preparation Time:
15 minutes

Cooking Time:
18 minutes

INGREDIENTS:

- 500 grams of cooked white rice
- 1 tablespoon water
- 1 tablespoon vegetable oil
- 2 teaspoons sesame oil, toasted and divided
- Salt and ground white pepper, as required
- Non-stick cooking spray
- 1 large egg, lightly beaten
- 75 grams frozen green peas, thawed
- 45 grams frozen carrots, thawed
- 1 teaspoon low-sodium soy sauce
- 1 teaspoon Sriracha sauce
- ½ teaspoon sesame seeds, toasted

INSTRUCTIONS:

1. In a large bowl, add the rice, water, vegetable oil, 1 teaspoon of sesame oil, salt, and white pepper and mix well.
2. Lightly grease the Air Fryer Pan with cooking spray and then slide inside.

3. Adjust the temperature of the Air Fryer to 195 °C to preheat for 5 minutes.
4. Press "Start/Pause" button to start preheating.
5. After preheating, place the rice mixture into the preheated Air Fryer Pan.
6. Slide the pan inside and set the time for 18 minutes.
7. Press "Start/Pause" button to start cooking.
8. After 6 minutes of cooking, press "Start/Pause" button to pause cooking.
9. Stir the rice mixture and press the "Start/Pause" button to resume cooking.
10. After 12 minutes of cooking, press "Start/Pause" button to pause cooking.
11. Place the beaten egg over the rice and press the "Start/Pause" button to resume cooking.
12. After 16 minutes of cooking, press "Start/Pause" button to pause cooking.
13. Add the peas and carrots to the pan with the rice mixture and stir to combine.
14. Again, press "Start/Pause" button to resume cooking.
15. Meanwhile, mix the soy sauce, Sriracha sauce, sesame seeds and the remaining sesame oil in a bowl.

16. After cooking time is finished, remove the rice mixture from Air Fryer and transfer it into a serving bowl.
17. Drizzle with the sauce mixture and serve.

....

 Per Serving:
Calories: 350 | **Fat:** 10g | **Carbs:** 54.7g | **Protein:** 8.1g

....

76. Roasted Peanuts

Servings:	Preparation Time:	Cooking Time:
4	10 minutes	15 minutes

INGREDIENTS:

- Non-stick cooking spray
- 150 grams of raw peanuts
- 2 teaspoons olive oil
- Salt, as required

INSTRUCTIONS:

1. Grease the Air Fryer Basket with cooking spray and then slide inside.
2. Adjust the temperature of the Air Fryer to 180 °C to preheat for 5 minutes.
3. Press "Start/Pause" button to start preheating.
4. After preheating, arrange the peanuts into the Air Fryer Basket.
5. Slide the basket inside and set the time for 15 minutes.
6. Press "Start/Pause" button to start cooking.
7. After 9 minutes of cooking, press "Start/Pause" button to pause cooking.
8. Transfer the peanuts into a large bowl.
9. Add the oil and salt and toss to coat well.
10. Return the peanuts into the Air Fryer Basket and insert them inside.
11. Again, press "Start/Pause" button to resume cooking.
12. After cooking time is finished, remove the peanuts from Air Fryer and transfer them into a large bowl.
13. Set aside to cool completely before serving.

 Per Serving:
Calories: 214 | Fat: 18.6g | Carbs: 6.1g | Protein: 9.7g

77. Roasted Cashews

Snacks Recipes

06

Servings:
8

 Preparation Time:
10 minutes

 Cooking Time:
5 minutes

 Servings:
4

 Preparation Time:
5 minutes

 Cooking Time:
10 minutes

INGREDIENTS:

- Non-stick cooking spray
- 260 grams of raw cashews
- One teaspoon of butter, melted
- Salt and ground black pepper, as required

INSTRUCTIONS:

1. In a bowl, mix all the ingredients.
2. Grease the Air Fryer Basket with cooking spray and then slide inside.
3. Adjust the temperature of the Air Fryer to 180 °C to preheat for 5 minutes.
4. Press "Start/Pause" button to start preheating.
5. After preheating, arrange the cashews into the Air Fryer Basket in a single layer.
6. Slide the basket inside and set the time for 5 minutes.
7. Press "Start/Pause" button to start cooking.
8. While cooking, shake the basket once halfway through.
9. After cooking time is finished, remove the cashews from Air Fryer and transfer them into a glass bowl.
10. Set aside to cool completely before serving.

 Per Serving:
Calories: 201 | Fat: 10g | Carbs: 11.2g | Protein: 16.4g

78. Spiced Chickpeas

INGREDIENTS:

- Non-stick cooking spray
- ½ (425-gram) can of chickpeas, rinsed and drained
- 2 teaspoons olive oil
- ¼ teaspoon ground cumin
- ¼ teaspoon cayenne powder
- ¼ teaspoon smoked paprika
- Salt, as required

INSTRUCTIONS:

1. Grease the Air Fryer Basket with cooking spray and then slide inside.
2. Adjust the temperature to 200 °C to preheat for 5 minutes.
3. Press "Start/Pause" button to start preheating.
4. In a bowl, add all the ingredients and toss to coat well
5. After preheating, arrange the chickpeas into the Air Fryer Basket in a single layer
6. Slide the basket inside and set the time for 10 minutes.
7. Press "Start/Pause" button to start cooking.
8. After cooking time is finished, remove the chickpeas from Air Fryer and serve.

 Per Serving:
Calories: 131 | Fat: 6.7g | Carbs: 15.5g | Protein: 5.9g

79. Carrot Sticks

Servings: 2 | **Preparation Time:** 15 minutes | **Cooking Time:** 12 minutes

Servings: 8 | **Preparation Time:** 15 minutes | **Cooking Time:** 30 minutes

INGREDIENTS:

- 1 carrot, peeled and cut into sticks
- 1 teaspoon olive oil
- 1 tablespoon fresh rosemary, finely chopped
- 1½ tablespoons white sugar
- ¼ teaspoon cayenne powder
- Salt and ground black pepper, as required

INSTRUCTIONS:

1. In a bowl, add all the ingredients and toss to coat well.
2. Grease the Air Fryer Basket with cooking spray and then slide inside.
3. Adjust the temperature of the Air Fryer to 200 ºC to preheat for 5 minutes.
4. Press "Start/Pause" button to start preheating.
5. After preheating, arrange the carrot sticks in the Air Fryer Basket in a single layer.
6. Slide the basket inside and set the time for 12 minutes.
7. Press "Start/Pause" button to start cooking.
8. After cooking time is finished, remove the carrot sticks from Air Fryer and serve hot.

 Per Serving:
Calories: 118 | **Fat:** 7.4g | **Carbs:** 14.5g | **Protein:** 0.4g

80. French Fries

INGREDIENTS:

- 795 grams of potatoes, peeled and cut into strips
- 60 millilitres olive oil
- 2 teaspoons paprika
- 1 teaspoon onion powder
- Non-stick cooking spray

INSTRUCTIONS:

1. Place the potato strips in a large bowl of water for about 1 hour.
1. Drain the potato strips well and pat them dry with paper towels.
2. Add the potato strips and the remaining ingredients to a large bowl and toss to coat well.
3. Grease the Air Fryer Basket with cooking spray and then slide inside.
4. Adjust the temperature to 190 ºC to preheat for 5 minutes.
5. Press "Start/Pause" button to start preheating.
6. After preheating, arrange the potato strips into the Air Fryer Basket in a single layer.
7. Slide the basket inside and set the time for 30 minutes.
8. Press "Start/Pause" button to start cooking.
9. After cooking time is finished, remove the French fries from Air Fryer and serve.

 Per Serving:
Calories: 132 | **Fat:** 7.3g | **Carbs:** 16.2g | **Protein:** 1.8g

81. Crispy Brinjal Slices

 Servings: 4

 Preparation Time: 15 minutes

 Cooking Time: 8 minutes

INGREDIENTS:

- 1 medium brinjal, peeled and cut into ½-inch round slices
- Salt, as required
- 60 grams of white flour
- 2 eggs, beaten
- 60 millilitres olive oil
- 120 grams of Italian-style breadcrumbs
- Non-stick cooking spray

INSTRUCTIONS:

1. In a colander, add the brinjal slices and sprinkle with salt.
2. Set aside for about 45 minutes
3. With paper towels, pat dries the brinjal slices.
4. Add the flour to a shallow dish.
5. Crack the eggs in a second dish and beat well.
6. In a third dish, mix the oil and breadcrumbs.
7. Coat each brinjal slice with flour, dip into beaten eggs, and then evenly coat with the breadcrumb mixture.
8. Grease the Air Fryer Basket with cooking spray and then slide inside.
9. Adjust the temperature of the Air Fryer to 200 °C to preheat for 5 minutes.
10. Press "Start/Pause" button to start preheating.
11. After preheating, arrange the brinjal slices in an Air Fryer Basket in a single layer.
12. Slide the basket inside and set the time for 8 minutes.
13. Press "Start/Pause" button to start cooking.
14. After cooking time is finished, remove the brinjal slices from Air Fryer and serve hot.

 Per Serving:
Calories: 354 | **Fat:** 18.4g | **Carbs:** 39.8g | Protein: 9.7g

82. Onion Rings

 Servings: 4

 Preparation Time: 15 minutes

 Cooking Time: 10 minutes

INGREDIENTS:

- 1 large onion, cut into 0.60-centimeters slices
- 160 grams of white flour
- 1 teaspoon baking powder
- Salt, as required
- 240 millilitres milk
- 1 egg
- 75 grams of dry breadcrumbs
- Non-stick cooking spray

INSTRUCTIONS:

1. Separate the onion slices into rings.
2. Mix the flour, baking powder, and salt in a shallow dish.
3. In a second dish, mix healthy milk and egg.
4. In a third dish, put the breadcrumbs.
5. Coat each onion ring with flour mixture, dip into egg mixture, and coat evenly with the breadcrumbs.
6. Grease the Air Fryer Basket with cooking spray and then slide inside.

7. Adjust the temperature to 185 °C to preheat for 5 minutes.
8. Press "Start/Pause" button to start preheating.
9. After preheating, arrange the onion rings into the Air Fryer Basket in a single layer.
10. Slide the basket inside and set the time for 7-10 minutes.
11. Press "Start/Pause" button to start cooking.
12. After cooking time is finished, remove the onion rings from Air Fryer and serve hot.

 Per Serving:
Calories: 285 | Fat: 3.8g | Carbs: 51.6g | Protein: 10.5g

83. Apple Chips

Servings:
2

Preparation Time:
10 minutes

Cooking Time:
8 minutes

INGREDIENTS:

- Non-stick cooking spray
- 1 apple, peeled, cored and thinly sliced
- 1 tablespoon white sugar
- ½ teaspoon ground cinnamon
- Pinch of ground cardamom
- Pinch of ground ginger
- Pinch of salt

INSTRUCTIONS:

1. Grease the Air Fryer Basket with cooking spray and then slide inside.
2. Adjust the temperature to 200 °C to preheat for 5 minutes.
3. Press "Start/Pause" button to start preheating.

4. In a bowl, add all the ingredients and toss to coat well.
5. After preheating, arrange the apple slices into the Air Fryer Basket in a single layer.
6. Slide the basket inside and set the time for 7-8 minutes.
7. Press "Start/Pause" button to start cooking.
8. After 4 minutes of cooking, press "Start/Pause" button to pause cooking.
9. Flip the apple slices and press the "Start/Pause" button to resume cooking.
10. After cooking time is finished, remove the apple chips from Air Fryer and serve.

 Per Serving:
Calories: 90 | Fat: 0.2g | Carbs: 24.1g | Protein: 0.4g

84. Tortilla Chips

Servings:
3

Preparation Time:
10 minutes

Cooking Time:
3 minutes

INGREDIENTS:

- Non-stick cooking spray
- 4 corn tortillas, cut into triangles
- 2 teaspoons olive oil
- Salt, as required

INSTRUCTIONS:

1. Grease the Air Fryer Basket with cooking spray and then slide inside.
2. Adjust the temperature of the Air Fryer to 200 °C to preheat for 5 minutes.
3. Press "Start/Pause" button to start preheating.

4. Coat the tortilla chips with oil and sprinkle with salt.
5. After preheating, arrange the tortilla triangles into the Air Fryer Basket in a single layer.
6. Slide the basket inside and set the time for 3 minutes.
7. Press "Start/Pause" button to start cooking.
8. After cooking time is finished, remove the tortilla chips from Air Fryer and transfer them into a large bowl.
9. Set aside to cool completely before serving.

 Per Serving:
Calories: 90 | **Fat:** 3.2g | **Carbs:** 14.3g | **Protein:** 1.8g

85. Mozzarella Sticks

Servings:
4

Preparation Time:
15 minutes

Cooking Time:
12 minutes

INGREDIENTS:

- 35 grams of white flour
- 3 tablespoons milk
- 455 grams mozzarella cheese block, cut into 7½x1¼-centimeters sticks
- 2 eggs
- 100 grams of plain breadcrumbs
- Non-stick cooking spray

INSTRUCTIONS:

1. In a shallow dish, place the flour.
2. In a second shallow dish, add the eggs and milk and beat well
3. In a third shallow dish, place the breadcrumbs.

4. Coat the mozzarella sticks with flour, then dip in egg mixture and finally, coat with the breadcrumbs
5. Arrange the mozzarella sticks onto a cookie sheet and freeze for about 1-2 hours.
6. Grease the Air Fryer Basket with cooking spray and then slide inside.
7. Adjust the temperature of the Air Fryer to 225 °C to preheat for 5 minutes.
8. Press "Start/Pause" button to start preheating.
9. After preheating, arrange the mozzarella sticks into the Air Fryer Basket in a single layer.
10. Slide the basket inside and set the time for 12 minutes.
11. Press "Start/Pause" button to start cooking.
12. After cooking time is finished, remove the mozzarella sticks from Air Fryer and set them aside to cool slightly.
13. Serve warm.

 Per Serving:
Calories: 255 | **Fat:** 9.3g | **Carbs:** 16.4g | **Protein:** 26.1g

86. Cheese Pastries

Servings:
6

Preparation Time:
15 minutes

Cooking Time:
5 minutes

INGREDIENTS:

- 1 egg yolk
- 115 grams feta cheese, crumbled
- 1 green onion, finely chopped

- 1 teaspoon fresh parsley, finely chopped
- Salt and ground black pepper, as required
- 2 frozen filo pastry sheets, thawed
- 2 tablespoons olive oil
- Non-stick cooking spray

INSTRUCTIONS:

1. In a large bowl, add the egg yolk, and beat well.
1. Add in the feta cheese, green onion, parsley, salt, and black pepper and mix well.
2. Cut each filo pastry sheet into three strips.
3. Add some of the feta mixtures to the underside of a strip
4. Fold the tip of the sheet over the filling in a zigzag manner to form a triangle.
5. Repeat with the remaining strips and fillings.
6. Grease the Air Fryer Basket with cooking spray and then slide inside.
7. Adjust the temperature to 200 °C to preheat for 5 minutes.
8. Press "Start/Pause" button to start preheating.
9. After preheating, arrange the pastries into the Air Fryer Basket in a single layer.
10. Slide the basket inside and set the time for 3 minutes.
11. Press "Start/Pause" button to start cooking.
12. After 3 minutes of cooking, adjust the temperature to 185 °C for 2 minutes.
13. After cooking time is finished, remove the pastries from Air Fryer and serve.

Per Serving:
Calories: 135 | Fat: 9.8g | Carbs: 8.1g | Protein: 4.2g

87. Potato Croquettes

Servings:	Preparation Time:	Cooking Time:
4	20 minutes	23 minutes

INGREDIENTS:

- 2 medium Russet potatoes, peeled and cubed
- 2 tablespoons white flour
- 1 egg yolk
- 55 grams Parmesan cheese, grated
- 2 tablespoons fresh chives, minced
- Pinch of ground nutmeg
- Salt and ground black pepper, as required
- 2 eggs
- 60 grams breadcrumbs
- 2 tablespoons vegetable oil
- Non-stick cooking spray

INSTRUCTIONS:

1. Add potatoes to the boiling water pan and cook for about 15 minutes.
2. Drain the potatoes well and transfer them into a large bowl.
3. With a potato masher, mash them and set them aside to cool completely.
4. In the same bowl of mashed potatoes, add the flour, Parmesan cheese, egg yolk, chives, nutmeg, salt, and black pepper and mix until well combined.
5. Make small equal-sized balls from the mixture.
6. Now, roll each ball into a cylinder shape
7. In a shallow dish, crack the eggs and beat well.
8. In another dish, mix the breadcrumbs and oil.
9. Dip the croquettes in egg mixture and then evenly coat with the breadcrumbs mixture.

10. Grease the Air Fryer Basket with cooking spray and then slide inside.
11. Adjust the temperature to 390 ºF to preheat for 5 minutes.
12. Press "Start/Pause" button to start preheating.
13. After preheating, arrange the croquettes into the Air Fryer Basket in a single layer.
14. Slide the basket inside and set the time for 7-8 minutes.
15. Press "Start/Pause" button to start cooking.
16. After cooking time is finished, remove the croquettes from Air Fryer and serve.

 Per Serving:
Calories: 297 | **Fat:** 14.2g | **Carbs:** 31.3g | **Protein:** 12.1g

88. Cod Sticks

Servings:
4

Preparation Time:
15 minutes

Cooking Time:
7 minutes

INGREDIENTS:

- 100 grams of white flour
- 4 eggs
- 2 garlic cloves, minced
- 1 green chilli, finely chopped
- 2 teaspoons light soy sauce
- Salt and ground black pepper, as required
- 3 (115-gram) skinless cod fillets, cut into rectangular pieces
- Non-stick cooking spray

INSTRUCTIONS:

1. In a shallow bowl, add the flour.

2. Add eggs, garlic, green chilli, soy sauce, salt, and black pepper to another bowl and mix well.
3. Coat each codpiece with flour and dip into the egg mixture.
4. Grease the Air Fryer Basket with cooking spray and then slide inside.
5. Adjust the temperature of the Air Fryer to 190 ºC to preheat for 5 minutes.
6. Press "Start/Pause" button to start preheating.
7. After preheating, arrange the cod pieces into the Air Fryer Basket in a single layer.
8. Slide the basket inside and set the time for 7 minutes.
9. Press "Start/Pause" button to start cooking.
10. After cooking time is finished, remove the carrot sticks from Air Fryer and serve warm.

 Per Serving:
Calories: 483 | **Fat:** 10.3g | **Carbs:** 38.3g | **Protein:** 55.3g

89. Buffalo Chicken Wings

Servings:
4

Preparation Time:
15 minutes

Cooking Time:
22 minutes

INGREDIENTS:

- 910 grams of chicken wings, cut into drumettes and flats
- 1 teaspoon chicken seasoning
- 1 teaspoon garlic powder
- Ground black pepper, as required
- Non-stick cooking spray

- 80 grams of red hot sauce
- 2 tablespoons low-sodium soy sauce
- 1 teaspoon olive oil

INSTRUCTIONS:

1. Sprinkle each chicken wing with chicken seasoning, garlic powder, and black pepper evenly.
2. Grease the Air Fryer Basket with cooking spray and then slide inside.
3. Adjust the temperature of the Air Fryer to 205 °C to preheat for 5 minutes.
4. Press "Start/Pause" button to start preheating.
5. Arrange the chicken wings into the Air Fryer Basket.
6. Slide the basket inside and set the time for 10 minutes.
7. Press "Start/Pause" button to start cooking.
8. While cooking, shake the basket once halfway through.
9. After cooking time is finished, remove the chicken wings from Air Fryer and transfer them into a bowl.
10. Drizzle with the hot sauce, oil, and soy sauce and toss to coat well.
11. Again, arrange the chicken wings into the Air Fryer Basket in a single layer and slide inside.
12. Adjust the temperature of the Air Fryer to 205 °C for 12 minutes.
13. Press "Start/Pause" button to start cooking.
14. After cooking time is finished, remove the chicken wings from Air Fryer and serve hot.

 Per Serving:
Calories: 313 | Fat: 13.6g | Carbs: 0.9g | Protein: 44.6g

90. Bacon-Wrapped

Shrimp

Servings:	Preparation Time:	Cooking Time:
6	15 minutes	7 minutes

INGREDIENTS:

- 455 grams bacon, thinly sliced
- 455 grams shrimp, peeled and deveined
- Non-stick cooking spray

INSTRUCTIONS:

1. Wrap each shrimp with one bacon slice.
2. Add the shrimp to a baking dish and refrigerate for about 20 minutes.
3. Grease the Air Fryer Basket with cooking spray and then slide inside.
4. Adjust the temperature to 390 °F to preheat for 5 minutes.
5. Press "Start/Pause" button to start preheating.
6. After preheating, arrange the shrimp into the Air Fryer Basket in a single layer.
7. Slide the basket inside and set the time for 5-7 minutes.
8. Press "Start/Pause" button to start cooking.
9. After cooking time is finished, remove the shrimp from Air Fryer and serve.

Per Serving:
Calories: 458 | Fat: 31.7g | Carbs: 1.1g | Protein: 40.3g

91. Banana Split

Servings:
2

Preparation Time:
15 minutes

Cooking Time:
16 minutes

INGREDIENTS:

- 3 tablespoons olive oil
- 120 grams of panko breadcrumbs
- 80 grams of corn flour
- 2 eggs
- 4 bananas, peeled and halved lengthwise
- 3 tablespoons white sugar
- ¼ teaspoon ground cinnamon
- Non-stick cooking spray
- 2 tablespoons walnuts, chopped

INSTRUCTIONS:

1. In a medium skillet, heat the oil over medium heat and cook breadcrumbs for about 3-4 minutes or until golden browned and crumbled, stirring continuously.
2. Transfer the breadcrumbs into a shallow bowl and set aside to cool.
3. In a second bowl, place the corn flour.
4. In a third bowl, whisk the eggs.
5. Coat the banana slices with flour and then dip into eggs and, finally, coat evenly with the breadcrumbs.
6. In a small bowl, mix the sugar and cinnamon.
7. Grease the Air Fryer Basket with cooking spray and then slide inside.
8. Adjust the temperature to 140 ºC to preheat for 5 minutes.
9. Press "Start/Pause" button to start preheating.
10. After preheating, arrange the banana slices into the Air Fryer Basket in a single layer and sprinkle with cinnamon sugar.
11. Slide the basket inside and set the time for 10 minutes.
12. Press "Start/Pause" button to start cooking.

Dessert Recipes

07

13. After cooking time is finished, remove the banana slices from Air Fryer and transfer the banana slices onto plates to cool slightly.
14. Sprinkle with chopped walnuts and serve.

 Per Serving:
Calories: 251 | **Fat:** 10.3g | **Carbs:** 29.2g | **Protein:** 4.1g

92. **Stuffed Apples**

Servings:
4

Preparation Time:
15 minutes

Cooking Time:
13 minutes

INGREDIENTS:

For Apples:

- 4 small firm apples, cored
- 75 grams of golden raisins
- 50 grams of blanched almonds
- 2 tablespoons white sugar
- Non-stick cooking spray

For Vanilla Sauce

- 120 grams of whipped cream
- 2 tablespoons white sugar
- 2½ millilitres vanilla extract

INSTRUCTIONS:

1. In a food processor, add the raisins, almonds, and sugar and pulse until chopped.
2. Carefully stuff each apple with a raisin mixture.
3. Grease the Air Fryer Basket with cooking spray and then slide inside.
4. Adjust the temperature of the Air Fryer to 180 ºF to preheat for 5 minutes.
5. Press "Start/Pause" button to start preheating.
6. After preheating, arrange the stuffed apples into the Air Fryer Basket
7. Slide the basket inside and set the time for 10 minutes.
8. Press "Start/Pause" button to start cooking.
9. Meanwhile, for the vanilla sauce: in a pan, add the cream, sugar, and vanilla extract over medium heat and cook for about 2-3 minutes or until sugar is dissolved, stirring continuously.
10. After cooking time is finished, remove the apples and transfer them onto plates to cool slightly.
11. Top with the vanilla sauce and serve.

 Per Serving:
Calories: 378 | **Fat:** 18.4g | **Carbs:** 54.7g | **Protein:** 5.4g

93. **Shortbread Fingers**

Servings:
10

Preparation Time:
15 minutes

Cooking Time:
12 minutes

INGREDIENTS:

- 75 grams caster sugar
- 170 grams of plain flour
- 170 grams butter
- ¼ teaspoon vanilla extract

INSTRUCTIONS:

1. In a large bowl, mix the sugar and flour.
2. Add the butter and vanilla extract and mix until a smooth dough forms.
3. Cut the dough into ten equal-sized fingers.
4. With a fork, lightly prick the fingers.
5. Slide the Air Fryer Basket inside and adjust the temperature to 180 °C to preheat for 5 minutes.
6. Press "Start/Pause" button to start preheating.
7. After preheating, arrange a piece of foil into the Air Fryer Basket.
8. Arrange fingers into the Air Fryer Basket in a single layer.
9. Slide the basket inside and set the time for 12 minutes.
10. Press "Start/Pause" button to start cooking.
11. After cooking time is finished, remove the shortbread fingers from Air Fryer and place them onto a wire rack to cool completely cool before serving.

 Per Serving:
Calories: 224 | **Fat:** 15g | **Carbs:** 22.6g | **Protein:** 2.3g

- 3 tablespoons powdered sugar
- Non-stick cooking spray

INSTRUCTIONS:

1. Arrange the tortillas onto a smooth surface.
2. Spread some strawberry jelly over each tortilla and top each with berries
3. Sprinkle each with powdered sugar.
4. Grease the Air Fryer Basket with cooking spray and then slide inside.
5. Adjust the temperature to 150 °C to preheat for 5 minutes.
6. Press "Start/Pause" button to start preheating.
7. After preheating, arrange the tortillas into the Air Fryer Basket.
8. Slide the basket inside and set the time for 5 minutes.
9. Press "Start/Pause" button to start cooking.
10. After cooking time is finished, remove the tortillas from Air Fryer and place them onto a platter to cool slightly.
11. Serve warm.

 Per Serving:
Calories: 212 | **Fat:** 0.9g | **Carbs:** 51.6g | **Protein:** 1.8g

94. Fruity Tacos

Servings:
2

Preparation Time:
10 minutes

Cooking Time:
5 minutes

INGREDIENTS:

- 2 soft shell tortillas
- 70 grams of strawberry jelly
- 50 grams blueberries
- 35 grams raspberries

95. Raspberry Cupcakes

Servings:
10

Preparation Time:
15 minutes

Cooking Time:
15 minutes

INGREDIENTS:

- 125 grams of self-rising flour

- ½ teaspoon baking powder
- Pinch of salt
- 15 grams cream cheese, softened
- 135 grams butter, softened
- 120 grams caster sugar
- 2 eggs
- 2 teaspoons fresh lemon juice
- 65 grams of fresh raspberries

INSTRUCTIONS:

1. In a bowl, mix flour, baking powder, and salt.
2. In another bowl, combine the cream cheese and butter.
3. Add the sugar and whisk until fluffy and light.
4. Now, place the eggs, one at a time and whisk until just combined.
5. Add the flour mixture and stir until well combined.
6. Stir in the lemon juice.
7. Place the mixture into silicon cups and top each with 2 raspberries.
8. Slide the Air Fryer Basket inside and adjust the temperature to 185 °C to preheat for 5 minutes.
9. Press "Start/Pause" button to start preheating.
10. After preheating, arrange the silicon cups into an Air Fryer Basket.
11. Slide the basket inside and set the time for 15 minutes.
12. Press "Start/Pause" button to start cooking.
13. After cooking time is finished, remove the silicone cups from Air Fryer and place them onto a wire rack to cool for about 10 minutes.
14. Now, invert the cupcakes onto a wire rack to completely cool before serving.

 Per Serving:

Calories: 209 | **Fat:** 12.5g | **Carbs:** 22.6g | **Protein:** 2.7g

96. Brownie Muffins

Servings:
12

Preparation Time:
15 minutes

Cooking Time:
12½ minutes

INGREDIENTS:

- Non-stick cooking spray
- 1 package fudge brownie mix
- 1 egg
- 90 millilitres of vegetable oil
- 2 teaspoons water
- 3 tablespoons walnuts, chopped

INSTRUCTIONS:

1. Grease 12 muffin moulds with cooking spray.
2. In a bowl, add all the ingredients and mix well.
3. Place mixture into the prepared muffin moulds.
4. Slide the Air Fryer Basket inside and adjust the temperature to 150 °C to preheat for 5 minutes.
5. Press "Start/Pause" button to start preheating.
6. After preheating, arrange the muffin moulds into the Air Fryer Basket.
7. Slide the basket inside and set the time for 10 minutes.
8. Press "Start/Pause" button to start cooking.
9. After cooking time is finished, remove the muffin moulds from Air Fryer and place

them onto a wire rack to cool for about 10 minutes.

10. Then invert the muffins onto a wire rack to completely cool before serving.

 Per Serving:
Calories: 241 | **Fat:** 9.6g | **Carbs:** 36.9g | **Protein:** 2.8g

97. Chocolate Soufflé

Servings:
2

Preparation Time:
10 minutes

Cooking Time:
16 minutes

INGREDIENTS:

- 85 grams semi-sweet chocolate, chopped
- 55 grams butter
- 2 eggs (yolks and whites separated)
- 3 tablespoons white sugar
- ½ teaspoon pure vanilla extract
- 2 tablespoons white flour
- Non-stick cooking spray
- 1 teaspoon powdered sugar plus extra for dusting

INSTRUCTIONS:

1. In a microwave-safe bowl, place the butter and chocolate and microwave on high heat for about 2 minutes or until melted completely, stirring after every 30 seconds.
2. Remove from microwave and stir the mixture until smooth.
3. In another bowl, add the egg yolks and beat well.
4. Add the sugar and vanilla extract and beat well.

5. Add the chocolate mixture and mix until well combined.
6. Add the flour and mix well.
7. Add the egg whites to a clean glass bowl and beat until soft peaks form.
8. Fold the whipped egg whites in 3 portions into the chocolate mixture
9. Grease 2 ramekins with cooking spray and then sprinkle each with a pinch of sugar.
10. Place mixture evenly into the prepared ramekins and smooth the top surface with the back of a spoon.
11. Slide the Air Fryer Basket inside and adjust the temperature to 165 °C to preheat for 5 minutes.
12. Press "Start/Pause" button to start preheating.
13. After preheating, arrange the ramekins into the Air Fryer Basket.
14. Slide the basket inside and set the time for 14 minutes.
15. Press "Start/Pause" button to start cooking.
16. After cooking time is finished, remove the ramekins from Air Fryer and set them aside to cool slightly.
17. Sprinkle with the powdered sugar and serve warm.

 Per Serving:
Calories: 602 | **Fat:** 39.4g | **Carbs:** 54g | **Protein:** 9.8g

98. Chocolate Cake

Servings:
6

Preparation Time:
15 minutes

Cooking Time:
25 minutes

INGREDIENTS:

- Non-stick cooking spray
- 130 grams of white flour
- 45 grams of cocoa powder
- 1 teaspoon baking powder
- ½ teaspoon baking soda
- Pinch of salt
- 130 grams of white sugar
- 120 grams of sour cream
- 115 grams butter, softened
- 3 eggs
- Two teaspoons of vanilla extract

INSTRUCTIONS:

1. Grease a cake pan with cooking spray.
2. Mix the flour, cocoa powder, baking powder, baking powder, baking soda, and salt in a large bowl.
3. Add the remaining ingredients and with an electric whisker, whisk on low speed until well combined.
4. Slide the Air Fryer Basket inside and adjust the temperature to 160 ºC to preheat for 5 minutes.
5. Press "Start/Pause" button to start preheating.
6. Place mixture into the prepared cake pan.
7. After preheating, arrange the cake pan into an Air Fryer Basket.
8. Slide the basket inside and set the time for 25 minutes.
9. Press "Start/Pause" button to start cooking.
10. After cooking time is finished, remove the cake pan from Air Fryer and place it onto a wire rack to cool for about 10 minutes.
11. Now, invert the cake onto a wire rack to cool completely before slicing.
12. Cut the cake into desired-sized slices and serve.

 Per Serving:
Calories: 393 | Fat: 23.1g | Carbs: 43.8g | Protein: 7.2g

99. Cherry Clafoutis

Servings:
4

Preparation Time:
15 minutes

Cooking Time:
25 minutes

INGREDIENTS:

- Non-stick cooking spray
- 332 grams of fresh cherries, pitted
- 45 millilitres vodka
- 35 grams of white flour
- 2 tablespoons white sugar
- Pinch of salt
- 120 grams of sour cream
- 1 egg
- 1 tablespoon butter
- 35 grams powdered sugar

INSTRUCTIONS:

1. Grease a cake pan with cooking spray.
2. In a bowl, mix the cherries and vodka.
3. In another bowl, combine the flour, sugar, and salt.
4. Add the sour cream and egg and mix until a smooth dough forms.
5. Place flour mixture evenly into the prepared cake pan.
6. Spread the cherry mixture over the dough.
7. Place butter on top in the form of dots.
8. Slide the Air Fryer Basket inside and adjust the temperature to 180 ºC to preheat for 5 minutes.
9. Press "Start/Pause" button to start preheating.

10. After preheating, arrange the cake pan into the Air Fryer Basket.

11. Slide the basket inside and set the time for 25 minutes.

12. Press "Start/Pause" button to start cooking.

13. After cooking time is finished, remove the cake pan from Air Fryer and place it onto a wire rack to cool for about 10 minutes.

14. Then invert the Clafoutis onto a platter and sprinkle with powdered sugar.

15. Cut the Clafoutis into desired-sized slices and serve warm.

 Per Serving:
Calories: 309 | Fat: 10.4g | Carbs: 45g | Protein: 3.5g

100. **Doughnuts Pudding**

Servings:
4

Preparation Time:
15 minutes

Cooking Time:
1 hour

INGREDIENTS:

- Six glazed doughnuts, cut into small pieces
- 170 grams s frozen sweet cherries
- 75 grams raisins
- 50 grams of white sugar
- 80 grams of semi-sweet chocolate chips
- 4 egg yolks
- 360 grams of whipping cream
- 1 teaspoon ground cinnamon

INSTRUCTIONS:

1. Mix doughnut pieces, cherries, raisins, chocolate chips, sugar, and cinnamon in a large bowl.

2. In another bowl, add the egg yolks and whipping cream and whisk until well combined.

3. Add the egg yolk mixture into the doughnut mixture and mix well.

4. Slide the Air Fryer Basket inside and adjust the temperature to 155 °C to preheat for 5 minutes.

5. Press "Start/Pause" button to start preheating.

6. Line a baking dish with a piece of foil.

7. Place the doughnut mixture evenly into the prepared baking dish.

8. After preheating, arrange the baking dish into an Air Fryer Basket.

9. Slide the basket inside and set the time for 60 minutes.

10. Press "Start/Pause" button to start cooking.

11. After cooking time is finished, remove the baking dish from Air Fryer and set it aside for about 5-10 minutes.

12. Serve warm.

 Per Serving:
Calories: 491 | Fat: 33.5g | Carbs: 46.3g | Protein: 5.3g

CONCLUSION

An Air Fryer is something to consider if you are in the market for a new kitchen appliance. They've become trendy in recent years due to their versatility and ability to cook food quickly and evenly. We hope this article has helped you learn more about what Air Fryers are and how they work and given some ideas for dishes you can make with one.

Thanks! Find your gift here!

My Mediterranean Air fryer cookbook in PDF.
An extensive collection of air fryer meals to have even more
Ideas, or make a gift. Send the Pdf to friends and family with
a single Click on Whatsapp or Social Network. Enjoy!

Pork and Lamb in the Air Fryer

Loin	55 Mins	360'F 182°C	(2 lbs.)
Pork Chops, bone In	12 Mins	400'F 204°C	(1-inch, 6.5 oz.)
Tenderloin	15 Mins	370'F 188°C	(1lb.)
Bacon	5 to 7 Mins	400'F 204°C	(regular)
Bacon	6 to10 Mins	400'F 204°C	thick cut}
Sausages	15 Mins	380"F 193°C	
Lamb LoinChops	8 to 12 Mins	400'F 204°C	(1-inch thick)
Rack of lamb	22 Mins	380"F 193°C	(1.5 - 2lbs.)

Chicken in the Air Fryer

Breast's bone	25 Mins	370'F 188°C	(1.25lbs.)
Breasts, boneless	12 Mins	380"F 193°C	(4 oz.)
Drumsticks	20 Mins	370F' 188°C	(2.5 lbs.)
Thighs, bone In	22 Mins	380"F 193°C	(2 lbs.)
Thighs, boneless	18 to 20 Mins	380"F 193°C	(1.5 lbs.)
Legs, bone In	30 Mins	380"F 193°C	(1.75lbs.)
Wings	12 Mins	400'F 204°C	(2 lbs.)
Game Hen	20 Mins	390"F 199°C	(halved- 2lbs.)
Whole Chicken	75 Mins	360'F 182°C	(6.5 lbs.)
Tenders	8 to 10 Mins	360'F 182°C	

COOKING TIME CHARTS

Beef in the Air Fryer

Burger	16 to 20 Mins	370' F 188°C	(4 oz.)
Flie! Mignon	18 Mins	400°F 204°C	(8 oz.)
Flank Steak	12 Mins	400'F 204°C	(1.5 lbs.)
London Broil	20 to 28 Mins	400'F 204°C	(2 lbs.)
Meatballs	7 Mins	380"F 193°C	1-inch}
Meatballs	10 Mins	380"F 193°C	(3-inch)
Rlbeye, bone In	10 to 15 Mins	400'F 204°C	1-inch, 8 oz.}
Sirloin steaks	9 to 14 Mins	400'F 204°C	1-inch,12 oz.}
Beef Eye Round Roast	45 to 55 Mins	390"F 199°C	(4lbs.)

Vegetables in the Air Fryer

Asparagus	5 Mins	400°F 204°C	(sliced 1-inch)
Beest	40 Mins	400°F 204°C	(whole)
Broccoli	6 Mins	400'F 204°C	(florets)
Brussels Sprouts	15 Mins	380"F 193°C	(halved)
Carrots	15 Mins	380"F 193°C	(sliced½-inch)
Cauliflower	12 Mins	400°F 204°C	(florets)
Com on the cob	6 Mins	390"F 199°C	
Eggplant	15 Mins	400°F 204°C	(1½-inch cubes)

Fennel	15 Mins	370'F 188°C	(quartered)
Green Beans	5 Mins	400°F 204°C	
Kale leaves	12 Mins	250'F 121°C	
Mushrooms	5 Mins	400F' 204°C	(sliced ¼-Inch)
Onions	10 Mins	400'F 204°C	(peart)
Parsnips	15 Mins	380"F 193°C	(½-inchchunks)
Peppers	15 Mins	400°F 204°C	(1-inchchunks)
Potatoes	15 Mins	400'F 204°C	(small baby, 1.5 lbs)
Potatoes	12 Mins	400°F 204°C	(1-inchchunks)
Potatoes	40 Mins	400'F 204°C	(baked whole)
Squash	12 Mins	400'F 204°C	(½-inchchunks)
Sweet Potato	30 to 35 Mins	380"F 193°C	(baked)
Tomatoe	4 Mins	400'F 204°C	(scherry)
Tomatoes	10 Mins	-18°C	(halves)
Zucchini	12 Mins	350'F 177°C	(½-inchsticks)

Printed in Great Britain
by Amazon

24892895R00051